THE LITTLE HISTORY OF ABERDEENSHIRE

THE LITTLE HISTORY OF ABERDEENSHIRE

DUNCAN HARLEY

The History Press

The White Rabbit put on his spectacles.
'Where shall I begin, please your Majesty,' he asked. 'Begin at the beginning,' the King said gravely,
'and go on till you come to the end. Then stop.'

Front cover: top, standing stone image by artist Margaret Maclean.

First published 2019
Reprinted 2020

The History Press
97 St George's Place,
Cheltenham, GL50 3QB
www.thehistorypress.co.uk

British Library Cataloguing in Publication Data.
A catalogue record for this book is available from the British Library.

ISBN 978 0 7509 8929 9

Typesetting and origination by The History Press
Printed in Turkey by Imak

CONTENTS

INTRODUCTION

Oddly belittled by best-selling Scottish crime novelist Alexander McCall Smith – author of *The No.1 Ladies' Detective Agency* – Aberdeenshire is, to the best of my knowledge, doing fine, despite the recent downturns in the price of oil. In a somewhat jocular speech at the launch of Bloody Scotland, a literary event celebrating the Scottish crime novel, McCall revealed that, 'If you want to get rid of characters in a serial novel, you have got to send them somewhere. I send any characters I don't want to write about anymore to Aberdeen. At least there they can freeze to death.'

Well, each to their own perhaps, although, when penning this introduction midway through the scorching summer of 2018 it was hard to make much sense of Smithies' dystopian aside.

In *The A–Z of Curious Aberdeenshire*, I exposed readers to a random series of tales from the north-east of Scotland. Factual stories about The Beatles' first tour of Aberdeenshire, a résumé of the career of sporting superstar Donald Dinnie, and a startling description of the 1916 terror-bombing of the village of Insch by a 300ft-long German Zeppelin sat side by side with mythological tales about the Maiden Stone at Crowmallie, the tomb of Eth the Swift-Foot at Kellands, and the mysterious mound of death at the Bass.

My intention in this new book is to provide the reader with a few more snippets from Aberdeenshire's colourful history. I have succumbed to the temptation to revisit some of the stories featured in my previous book and trust that I will be forgiven for expanding greatly on those tales. The Blenheim of Buchan, a full exposé of the Aberdeen typhoid scandal, plus an expanded tale of artist–priest Peter Anson's life in the north-east are examples.

Tales about the Beaker People, those blue-painted warriors of ancient Pictland and the northern invasions of the men from Rome lead the reader gently through the early history of the area. Stories of bloody battles, agricultural improvements, wars and industrial revolution bring us up to the present day where, instead of taking to arms on gore-splattered battlefields, Aberdonians are willing participants in that economic game sometimes termed the hunt for black gold. Along the way there are a couple of twentieth-century conflicts and tales of religious and economic change. In short, *The Little History of Aberdeenshire* begins at the beginning and ends at the end, at least as we know it so far. As for the actual county of Aberdeenshire, where does it begin and indeed where does it end? Local government boundaries and parliamentary constituency lines change with the winds of political whim and in past times county boundaries were quite uncertain. I have tried, where practicable, to keep within current political boundaries; however, please forgive the occasional foreign foray into the ancient lands of Greater Grampian. Those pesky Romans and those proudly possessive Picts cared little about such petty boundary restrictions. The labels Aberdeenshire, the north-east and Grampian are variously used to refer to the County of Aberdeenshire within this volume. As always, please enjoy these wee snippets from history. Please dip into these pages and smile gently on the past.

Duncan Harley

ACKNOWLEDGEMENTS

I am as always indebted to both the oral and written recollections of the people of the north-east of Scotland. There are many splendid publications out there that record the local history from the perspective of the folk on the land or beside the shore who talked the talk and lived the life. Often published in tiny editions by local printers, more used perhaps to turning out batches of Christmas, birthday or communion cards, they are often read by a very small audience. Toulmin, Christie, Anson, McConnachie and Smith are just a few of the local authors who have left us an unrivalled legacy. Then there is Tacitus, who left us a quite splendid account of how the Romans fought against the Picts. He failed to record the actual location of that battle he called Mons Graupius, but most accounts place it squarely in the Garioch and who am I to disagree.

I have, where possible, referenced these local writers in the bibliography and I am, as always, indebted to the staff at Aberdeenshire Library Service for their enthusiastic support throughout the writing process.

I am also indebted to Paul Kohn, Mike Shepherd and *Aberdeen Voice* editor Fred Wilkinson for their encouragement, and to Lewis-based artist Margaret Maclean who contributed images. As always, my partner Janice Rayne has encouraged the writing and I am grateful for her support in the making of this new collection of Aberdeenshire tales.

ABERDEENSHIRE

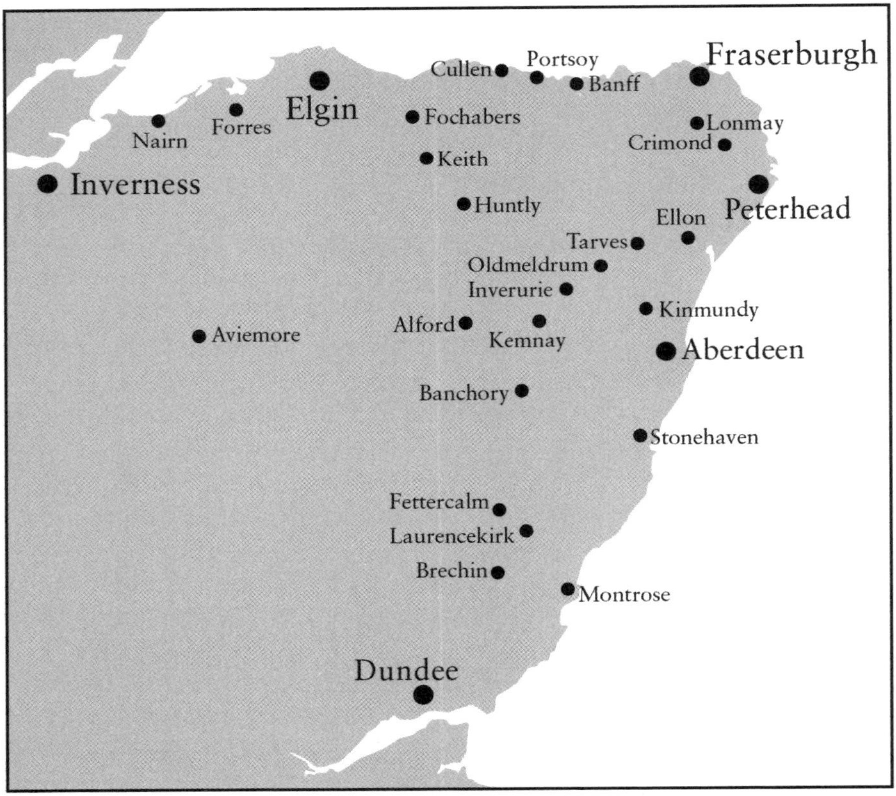

1

EARLY TIMES

Stanley Kubrick's cult science-fiction movie *2001: A Space Odyssey* turned fifty in the May of 2018 and, with an opening scene portraying the dawn of man, suggested that the human intellect is underpinned by a marked propensity for violence. In the iconic 'Dawn of Man' sequence, an ape-person is seen picking up a thigh bone to assert his dominance. However, current thinking might suggest that those weaponised bones were more likely to have been used in subsistence agriculture as tools for the breaking open of virgin ground rather than for the breaking open of human heads. Aberdeenshire's scattered museums sport an unrivalled collection of such ancient artefacts and the region's landscape hosts ancient sites rivalling Stonehenge. A proliferation of Pictish symbol stones, some ancient long barrows and a good few Beaker People burial cists hold clues to the activity of the early inhabitants of the north-east landscape.

Oddly perhaps, public works such as the recently completed Aberdeen Western Peripheral Route – better known by the acronym AWPR – and groundworks for the A96 Kintore bypass have allowed researchers a unique window into that past.

A local history conference hosted by Aberdeen City Library Service at the Beach Ballroom in early 2017 featured a talk by Bruce Mann, Regional Archaeologist at Aberdeenshire Council. Alongside describing the archaeological history of the county, Bruce made clear the dilemma that faces those who look into the past. Historians are well aware of the pitfalls facing them – revisionist takes on history are mandatory. Today's take on history may not stand the test of time and seemingly the same applies to archaeology. With over 29,000 recorded historic sites in the north-east of Scotland to oversee, the council Indiana Jones team are constantly having to re-evaluate the archaeological record of the county in the light of a torrent of new finds.

Often, exploration of sites associated with new development provides the catalyst for re-examination of what Bruce describes as 'what we thought we knew' and the finds associated with the £745m, 28-mile-long AWPR left the archaeological team stunned. Not only did excavations associated with the construction of the ring road unearth structures and artefacts dating back to 15,000 BC, but fresh evidence relating to the Roman occupation of the area came to light in the form of the discovery of around ninety Roman bread ovens at Milltimber. The uncovering of these ovens, dating from around AD 84, mirrored previous discoveries made in the course of an archaeological excavation undertaken between September 2003 and March 2004 prior to a proposed housing development at Deer's Den Kintore. Used to bake a kind of flatbread similar to pizza, probably topped off with locally sourced vegetables, the Roman-era ovens uncovered at Kintore would have no doubt been used to sustain the thousands of foreign troops stationed in the area during the course of the Romano–Scottish campaigns.

Approximately 4.65ha of the site was carefully explored and alongside twenty-one Roman ovens found within a section of Roman marching camp, evidence of early prehistoric (Neolithic and Early Bronze Age) and later prehistoric (Late Bronze Age and Iron Age) settlement was recorded. Additionally, alongside the Roman archaeology of conquest, a number of Bronze Age roundhouses were uncovered. Archaeologists suspect that these would have been built of wattle and daub with perhaps a beehive roof and an upper and lower floor with domesticated animals occupying the lower level.

Commenting on the Aberdeen Western Peripheral Route archaeological finds, Bruce Mann suggests that many of the finds raise more questions than answers. 'They push back known human activity in the region by at least 2,000 years,' he says, 'and add new detail to how our ancestors lived and died.' In addition, the sheer scale of the Roman-era archaeological find reveals a completely new dimension to the story of Rome's attempts to subdue the rebellious population of the area.

A highlight from the AWPR excavations was an intact Beaker pot dating from around 2000 BC. Named after the distinctive ceramic pots often found within their burial cists, the Beaker People are thought to have settled in Britain around 2000 BC, having migrated north from the Netherlands. Beaker burials typically take the form of short stone-lined cists around 4ft long. The body was placed on one side with the limbs bent into a foetal position. Typical accompanying grave goods included tools and ornaments possibly intended to be used in an afterlife, and in some cases a layer of sand or pebbles was laid in the bottom of the cist.

The highly decorated ceramic pots found within many Beaker People cists display an intricate white decorative infill that, on analysis, often proves to be a pigment derived from cremated ground up bones. Whether these pigments are made from animal or human bones is unclear, but it may be that the practice had a ceremonial or symbolic origin.

Additionally, research indicates that gender played a role in the alignment of the corpse. Graves examined by archaeologists from the University of Aberdeen revealed that male remains were typically aligned with the head facing east, while female remains often had the body placed with the head facing west. The reasons for this practice are unknown and, as with the mystery of the bone pigment, the secrets and beliefs associated with this gender-based alignment vanished along with the last of the Beaker folk.

STANDING STONE CIRCLES

Stone circles can be found across the UK and mainland Europe. Fine examples can be seen at Callanish on the Isle of Lewis, at Stenness near Kirkwall and of course at Stonehenge. Aberdeenshire plays host to around 10 per cent of all the stone circles recorded in the UK and many of the region's circles are of a design unique to the area. Described in the literature as Recumbent Stone Circles, these rank amongst the oldest man-made structures in Scotland. Built perhaps 4,000 years ago, these constructions are termed recumbent since, although made up of standing stones arranged in circular form, they typically feature one giant boulder, weighing anything between 1.5 and 45 tons, laid on the flat with two flanking upright stones on either side. Often termed altar stones, these recumbents usually feature on the south-west part of the circle, leading to speculation that the structures were used to record the passing seasons or the passage of the sun and the moon. Some have little hollows known as cup marks, assumed by many to have been carved in order to drain away blood from human or animal sacrifices; however, often the cup marks are carved on the sides instead of on the horizontal surfaces of the stones, making them quite unsuitable for holding blood or indeed any other liquid.

Standing Stone Circle (© Margaret MacLean)

Loudon Wood Standing Stones (© Duncan Harley)

Despite a superstitious belief in some parts of the county that these circles were used for heathen worship and are therefore likely to have supernatural significance, many standing stone sites have been robbed piecemeal with the ancient artefacts ending up in the walls of farm steadings, the foundations of buildings and in drystone dykes. There are even some built into the sides of Christian churches such as Fyvie's St Peter's Kirk, where a trio of Pictish symbol stones and a Pictish cross are built into the east gable. The church authorities must have been unafraid of disturbing such sites but there are countless folktales of local farmers who, having appropriated standing stones for use in construction projects, quickly returned the monoliths to their point of origin following a period of bad luck. Death, bankruptcy and misfortune seemingly followed the desecrations. Despite this, many sites have been completely dismantled over the centuries and have disappeared from the landscape forever.

AIKEY BRAE STONE CIRCLE

In a tourist guide to ten of the 'best stone circles in Aberdeenshire', Aberdeenshire Council list Aikey Brae, Easter Aquhorthies and Loanhead of Daviot as being worthy of mention. The Aikey Brae circle is today partially hidden within forestry but is relatively intact. Situated in the heart of the Buchan countryside just off the B9029 between New Deer and Maud, Aikey was until a just a few decades ago the focus of an annual horse fair attracting a great many of the Scottish traveller community. Alongside the horse dealing there were trinkets, tin-ware and no doubt an abundance of lucky white heather for sale. Cornkister George Morris recalled the scene in a vinyl recording of the ballad 'The Horse Fair at Aikey' for the Beltona label:

For at Aikey Brae, Aikey Brae,
Aff we set on the Sabbath day;
And the sicht was enough tae pit hens aff their lay,
On the day we gaed tae Aikey.
There wis motor cars and charabancs,
Dakers gigs and caravans,
Auld folks in Fordies and bairnies in prams,
Aa on the road tae Aikey.

And when we landed at the Brae,
I stood and I glowert in great dismay,
I said, 'Can this the Sabbath day?'
On the day we gaed tae Aikey Brae.
There were fishers fae Buckie and trawlers fae Mull,
Herrin gutters fae Torry and sailors fae Hull;
Pick-pockets and sharpers, the saft mans tae gull,
At the Sunday fair at Aikey.

Fairm Jocks and their Jeanies, they come tae the fair,
And lairds fae the castle, their kilted knees fair,

The tramps and the hawkers enjoyed themselves there,
At the Sunday fair at Aikey Brae.
An evangelist singing oot Happy Days,
Stand next til a fiddler playing Clean Pease Strae,
While Bashin the Bruiser saying, 'Ye'll step this way,'
At the Sunday fair at Aikey.

Cheap johns and flash doctors in grand array,
Were daein a roarin trade that day,
I may be auld fashioned but still I wad say,
Fit way its allowed on a Sabbath day.

The horse trading aspect of the ancient fair had pretty much petered out by the mid-1950s. However, Aberdeen resident Janice Rayne recalls that 'when we lived in Maud during the 1950s and 1960s we attended the fair and even made a point of going back each year long after we moved to Stonehaven. There was a marquee dance on the Friday and another on the Saturday. Although there were still a good few horses for sale in and around the showground, the main attraction was the funfair which included a rib-tickler, sideshows and sometimes a Wall of Death.'

Maud resident Avril Wilson recalls how a relative lost her false teeth amongst the sideshows. 'When you went into the rotating barrel, the floor dropped and the centrifugal force kind of stuck you to the side of the ride. My aunty opened her mouth too quick one time while on the ride and her false teeth were launched out of her mouth never to be found again.'

No doubt the ancients at the stone circle on the summit of Parkhouse Hill above the Aikey Brae travellers' site would have watched proceedings with great interest. Today the nine whinstone and granite uprights plus the 30-ton recumbent stone that form the 14m diameter circle are rarely visited and the casual walker is likely to have the place completely to themselves.

Aikey, although off the tourist track, may be the most intact Neolithic/Bronze Age circle in the whole of Buchan and J.B. Pratt, a Victorian historian and author, commented as far back as 1858 that it was 'one of the very few circles that the utilitarian hand of agricultural improvement has spared'.

EASTER AQUHORTHIES STONE CIRCLE

The ancient standing stones at Easter Aquhorthies, on the outskirts of Inverurie, appear to have been chosen specifically for their colour. A mixture of red jasper and grey granite uprights sit alongside a humongous recumbent boulder quarried from the foot of nearby Bennachie. Described by Historic Environment Scotland as, 'An intact, recumbent stone circle consisting of eleven erect stones, the recumbent stone and three stones set almost at right angles to it, all set in a low ridge of small boulders', Easter Aquhorthies attracts a steady stream of visitors keen to touch the monoliths. Seemingly red jasper has spiritual qualities and, as a result, portions of some stones have been rubbed smooth over the centuries.

This ancient Neolithic circle is, even nowadays, relatively complete and today attracts what unkind locals describe as 'folk intent on watching the mid-summer dawn while performing fertility rights and Mother Earth ceremonies'. The *circa* 4,000-year-old site is a popular backdrop for wedding photographers and on more than a few occasions loving couples have exchanged wedding vows alongside the ancient Moon Stone. Indeed, one bride, a local postie, recently arrived at the ancient altar in a red-liveried postal delivery van to make her heavenly vows under the watchful eye of the ancient gods.

The name Easter Aquhorthies probably derives from the Gaelic language but opinions differ as to the exact meaning.

Some believe that it means field of prayer while others contend that it refers to a 'field of the pillar stone' from the Gaelic *achadh choirthe*. Either way, the place certainly reeks of old-time religious and new-age metaphysical significance.

LOANHEAD OF DAVIOT STONE CIRCLE

The recumbent stone circle at Loanhead of Daviot is worthy of special mention. Subject of a meticulous excavation in 1932, this circle sits just a few hundred yards north of the village of Daviot, north of Inverurie. The lower 9-acre portion of the site is now occupied by a Scout Association campsite and consists of rough woodland. The upper part of the hill, however, holds possibly the most thoroughly investigated recumbent stone circle in the entire north-east.

Described by Historic Environment Scotland as being around 20.5m in diameter and formed of eight standing stones, two flankers plus a massive frost-split, recumbent stone, the site shows evidence of continual use over an extended period of time. According to the New Statistical Account for Scotland, there were originally two such sites at Daviot. One lay some 800 yards down the brae in the old kirkyard and was completely destroyed in around 1820 by an enthusiastic local clergyman. The surviving circle was excavated, documented and to some extent reconstructed by H.E. Kilbride Jones in 1928 and he records the progress of his investigations in a somewhat ponderously titled paper: 'An account of the excavation of the stone circle at Loanhead of Daviot and of the standing stones of Cullerlie, Echt, both in Aberdeenshire, on behalf of HM Office of Works'.

Disparaging of so-called amateur archaeologists, Kilbride writes, 'Past investigators, if they were scientifically inclined, have concerned themselves with a series of trial trenches within the area of the main circle; while others, with less laudable ideals, have pillaged the centre to satisfy their own curiosity.' Kilbride was firmly in the scientifically-inclined category; his diligent approach to digging up the remnants of the past makes for interesting if somewhat difficult reading. Suffice it to say that the man and his team found literally thousands of artefacts ranging from tiny fragments of Beaker earthenware to sharp shards of what may have been Roman-era pottery and that he describes every single one of these finds in meticulous detail. His report is nothing if not precise.

An almost complete ceramic item that he describes as an 'Incense Cup Urn' was discovered under a pile of calcined human bone and he records that, 'The collection of Iron Age pottery from the stone circle at Loanhead is truly remarkable on account of its variety, and nothing comparable in numbers has hitherto been found upon the mainland of Scotland.'

A feature of his investigation was the identification of the original pits that housed the five or so toppled stones he encountered during his excavations. Using only a 1-ton block and tackle and some compliant students, he succeeded in raising the fallen monoliths back into place. Uprights weighing in at as much as 5 tons were re-erected using these methods and Kilbride concluded that his scientifically calculated reconstruction mirrored the methods of the builders of the original *circa* 1800 BC stone circle.

ROMANS BEARING ARMS

At its zenith, the Roman Empire stretched from North Africa all the way to Scotland. Aberdeenshire marked the northernmost boundary of Roman influence in Britain but the occasional forays north into the land of the Celts proved costly in terms of both manpower and resources, and eventually the Roman legions, recognising perhaps that they were at the very limits of conquest, withdrew southwards.

Imperial Rome then concentrated on Romanising a more compliant southern Britain. Defensive structures such as Hadrian's Wall (*circa* AD 122) and Agricola's line of forts along the Antonine Wall (*circa* AD 142) marked the true northern frontiers of the Roman Empire and there is little evidence, apart from an extensive series of temporary marching camps, of any permanent occupation of north-east Scotland. Aberdeenshire boasts no Roman roads and, to date at least, no Roman villas have been uncovered.

Until quite recently, very few of Aberdeenshire's Roman marching camps were known to archaeologists but with the advent of aerial surveying techniques during the twentieth century, a much more comprehensive picture of the true extent of the Roman presence was revealed. For example, in 1975, during the course of an aerial reconnaissance flight from Perth to the Moray Firth, a Roman camp was discovered at Durno just north of Inverurie and strategically sited alongside the River Urie between Old Rayne and Pitcaple. At 57 hectares, this previously unknown archaeological site proved, following ground surveys, to be the largest temporary camp then known in the north-east. Indeed, some accounts – such as that of *Grampian Battlefields* author Peter Marren – suggest that the Durno camp was large enough to have housed up to 20,000 troops.

Built to withstand a determined enemy assault, these camps were established in just a few hours to a standardised design and often at the end of a long day's march. With a perimeter ditch and perhaps a palisade erected from prefabricated materials, they provided both a defensive structure for the occupying troops and, of course, a jumping-off point for assaults on nearby enemy strongholds.

Another such camp, dating from the first-century AD, sits high on the grassy hillside above the coastal town of Stonehaven. Arguably one of the finest examples of a marching camp in the whole of Scotland, the Roman camp at Raedykes, just off the Slug Road, occupies some 38 hectares and once housed several thousand troops. Kempstone Hill, to the east of Raedykes, was once a favoured location for the Battle of Mons Graupius. However, debate continues as to the location of the actual battle site and little in the way of Roman artefacts appears to have been unearthed in the area, although a Roman coin hoard, including some denarii dating from the time of Septimius Severus (*circa* AD 211), was found on nearby Cowie Common in 1843.

In AD 79 Agricola, then Roman governor of Britannia, sent a fleet to survey Scotland's coast. As Agricola's forces advanced, conquering southern Scotland by AD 83, the Caledonian tribes faced imminent invasion. According to the Roman historian Tacitus, the Caledonians then 'turned to armed resistance on a very large scale', attacking Roman strongpoints and skirmishing amongst the hills and the glens of the disputed territory. A vengeful Rome was not at all pleased.

MONS GRAUPIUS – A BATTLE TOO FAR

In his circa AD 98 biography of his father-in-law Agricola, Tacitus records amongst other things the victory of the Roman general Agricola's armies over the Barbarian hordes of Caledonia. Much has been made of the fact that, although Tacitus goes on at length about the battle, he fails to pin down exactly where the clash actually took place.

What is clear, however, is that the tussle took place in AD 83 during the sixth year of Agricola's campaign to conquer the rebellious blue-painted naked northerners. Tacitus tantalisingly records that at a place he calls Mons Graupius the Caledonians made the fatal error of confronting the Roman army head-on. Not a good idea by any means. The Roman army was well used to taking on undisciplined tribal hordes and had a well-documented track record of defeating rebellious nations in battle. A quick stab with a gladius normally put paid to the enemy front ranks and as the blood and the gore flowed, the legionaries moved forward under strict discipline and with the secure knowledge that the Roman war machine was capable of grinding any enemy into the ground.

Then, of course, they met the Picts. The Picts were probably technologically equal to the Romans in many ways. Few written records remain; however, the archaeological records include an item termed the Deskford Carnyx (*c.* 300 BC). Described by The National Museums Scotland as an Iron Age trumpet, the sheet bronze and brass, wooden tongued and enamel eyed carnyx was unearthed in a peat bog at Deskford near Banff in far off 1816.

Today only the head survives and the ancient object lacks the erect crest, ears, enamelled eyes, wooden tongue and long cylindrical tube that it once boasted. Carried into battle in the face of a Roman army, the thunderous blast of the woodwind instrument must have been completely terrifying.

More used to easy victories, the Romans decided that enough was enough. Rome had met its northern nemesis and in a decisive move the mighty legions retreated south to take up defensive positions behind the Antonine Wall.

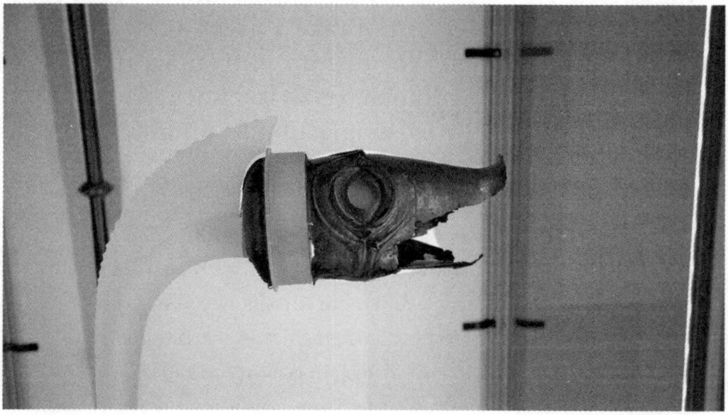

Deskford Carnyx (© Duncan Harley)

There are at least a dozen contenders for the actual location of the Mons Graupius battlefield, ranging from the site of the present-day golf course at Gleneagles near Auchterarder to Culloden's Drumossie Moor – site of the very last pitched battle, discounting Thatcher's 1984 campaign against the National Union of Mineworkers, to be fought on mainland British soil.

Buchan's Mormond Hill and Raedykes at Stonehaven are also strong contenders for the Graupius battle but no one alive today has a solid clue as to the actual location. The scholars and archaeologists will no doubt solve the thorny issue in the fullness of time but one location in Aberdeenshire ticks a good few of the boxes.

BENNACHIE

The Bennachie hill range lies to the north of Inverurie and is just a few miles from the Roman marching camp at Durno. Tacitus mentions a prominent hill as a backdrop and the 1698ft peak of the Mither Tap of Bennachie certainly fits this description. Additionally, the gently sloping plateau along the eastern side of the hill offers ample space for a pitched battle and it does not take a great leap of faith to imagine a Roman army formed up in front of the Durno camp enticing the Caledonian forces to attack.

Tacitus describes the ensuing action in suitably dramatic prose:

> At first the action was carried on at a distance. The Britons, armed with long swords and short targes, with steadiness and dexterity avoided or struck down our missile weapons, and at the same time poured in a torrent of their own. Agricola then encouraged three Batavian and two Tungrian cohorts to fall in and come to close quarters; a method of fighting familiar to these veteran soldiers, but embarrassing to the enemy from the nature of their

armour; for the enormous British swords, blunt at the point, are unfit for close grappling, and engaging in a confined space. When the Batavians; therefore, began to redouble their blows, to strike with the bosses of their shields, and mangle the faces of the enemy; and, bearing down all those who resisted them on the plain, were advancing their lines up the ascent; the other cohorts, fired with ardor and emulation, joined in the charge, and overthrew all who came in their way: and so great was their impetuosity in the pursuit of victory, that they left many of their foes half dead or unhurt behind them. In the meantime, the troops of cavalry took to flight, and the armed chariots mingled in the engagement of the infantry; but although their first shock occasioned some consternation, they were soon entangled among the close ranks of the cohorts, and the inequalities of the ground. Not the least appearance was left of an engagement of cavalry; since the men, long keeping their ground with difficulty, were forced along with the bodies of the horses; and frequently, straggling chariots, and affrighted horses without their riders, flying variously as terror impelled them, rushed obliquely athwart or directly through the lines. Those of the Britons who, yet disengaged from the fight, sat on the summits of the hills, and looked with careless contempt on the smallness of our numbers, now began gradually to descend; and would have fallen on the rear of the conquering troops, had not Agricola, apprehending this very event, opposed four reserved squadron of horse to their attack, which, the more furiously they had advanced, drove them back with the greater celerity. Their project was thus turned against themselves; and the squadrons were ordered to wheel from the front of the battle and fall upon the enemy's rear. A striking and hideous spectacle now appeared on the plain: some pursuing; some striking; some making prisoners, whom they slaughtered as others came in their way. Now, as their several dispositions prompted, crowds of armed Britons fled before inferior numbers, or a few, even unarmed, rushed upon their foes, and offered themselves to a voluntary death. Arms, and carcasses, and mangled limbs, were promiscuously strewed, and the field was dyed in blood.

Tacitus's vivid account of the Roman victory concludes that a quite staggering total of 10,000 Picts were killed in the battle. He records, however, that the good guys – the Romans – lost a mere 360 men. In the splendid tradition of Paul Brickhill's Second World War classic *The Great Escape*, there is no mention of any wounded. It was, of course, quite common for Roman writers to overstate enemy casualties and the practice of overstating victory continues to this day. Occupying forces in the various twentieth- and twenty-first-century conflicts in Iraq and Afghanistan proved adept at obscuring the body count and claiming territorial conquest where no such ground was ever won.

Even a cursory examination of the tactical worth of the victory at Mons Graupius leads one to the conclusion that Agricola's advance into the territory that we now call Aberdeenshire was at best a hollow victory. There is little doubt that the Romans were victorious and Tacitus' account confirms that the Caledonians were scattered on the field. But, following the victory, the Romans headed back south. It was late in the year and the campaigning season had ended. Agricola was recalled to Rome soon afterwards and none of the military leaders who succeeded him were to have much success in conquering the north-east of Scotland or indeed any of the territory north of the Antonine Wall. In reality, Mons Graupius represented nothing more than a bloody skirmish on the northern fringes of the Roman Empire.

SUMMER WANDERERS

A quick glance around the period between the strategic retreat of the Romans from Aberdeenshire and the arrival of the Bravehearts reveals a good few tales about the Celts, the Norsemen and, of course, the Anglo–Normans. When Agricola invaded Aberdeenshire it was already occupied by a good few independent tribes. Those little kingdoms, such as Pictland and Dalriada, often fought amongst themselves but none could gain the upper hand for long. Eventually, in around AD 844, King Kenneth MacAlpin appears to have gained a measure of overall control. His kingdom extended at least as far as Lothian and his grandson Duncan became the first king of Scotland in 1034.

The kings of the time often relied on booty from conquest to bolster their position and battles won provided a rich harvest of both gold and land. Since Duncan's kingdom did not extend to the Western Isles or indeed the northern mainland of Scotland, it remained vulnerable to attack from Norsemen. These seaborne foreigners often raided the Buchan coastline and places such as Cullen and Peterhead boast lurid tales recording battles won and battles lost. Around AD 954, for example, a party of Norse raiders made landfall near Cruden. The exact battle site is nowadays obscure but perhaps the aptly named Summer Wanderers were defeated by determined locals on the steep slopes of the Aldie Hill near Cruden Bay.

The Scandinavians attacked again in 1004, at which time the Moray coastal village of Gamrie was raided. On this occasion, the Norsemen were defeated and the skulls of three of their leaders are reputed to be interred within the walls of the local church. Along the coast at Cullen, the local golf course was the site of a later Scandinavian invasion. Described by *Golf Monthly* as 'the epitome of quirky, a course like no other', the present-day clubhouse sits alongside the Three Kings rock stack, which is reputed to mark the graves of three Norse pirate leaders who died violently in that seaside skirmish.

North-east writer Doris Davidson based her romantic novel *The Three Kings* at Cullen, with the lead character, the orphaned Katie Mair, renaming the rock stacks as The Three Wise Men – her trusted friends and the only ones to whom she could tell her troubles.

Cullen, alongside its well-known association with Davidson's kings, is also associated with Cullen Skink. This is a hearty chowder-like soup whose main ingredients are smoked haddock, potatoes and milk with maybe a leek and some onion thrown in for good measure, the town is famous for it and rightly so. Even the road signs on the outskirts of town proclaim 'Welcome to the Royal Burgh of Cullen. Home of Cullen Skink', and the Cullen Bay Hotel proudly hosts the annual Cullen Skink World Championship. The 2013 event was won by local chef Tracey Fuller using her very own recipe, which included some so-called 'secret ingredients', leading the judging panel to award her the winner's crown against stiff opposition from nearby Portsoy.

After the Viking invaders left, the north-east tale turns to the likes of Macbeth. In 1057 or so, there was a violent dispute regarding the kingship of Scotland and, in a surprise attack, Malcolm Canmore defeated Macbeth during a running fight just north of Lumphanan. The precise battle site is now obscured by time although locals sometimes point gullible tourists towards Macbeth's Well, Macbeth's Cairn and, of course, the local hostelry, The Macbeth Arms.

The murdered – some say decapitated – Macbeth now lies alongside a dozen or so monarchs in a graveyard full of Scottish kings on the west coast island of Iona.

Not much is really known about Macbeth although Shakespeare took a good stab at the tale. The years separating Dunsinane from Macbeth's final appearance in the mythology surrounding the man are largely unrecorded. All that can really be said is that he was crowned king following an alliance with a Viking ruler of Orkney, was probably extremely homicidal, and may have lost his head during the skirmish at Lumphanan. More than that is pure speculation and the Shakespearian myth is nothing more than an attempt to capitalise on legend. Even the three witches, originally from further south, are perhaps a local invention, although in truth a trio of female sorcerers were found guilty and put to death in Lumphanan in some forgotten year or other.

Indeed, Lumphanan and the nearby parishes of Leochel Cushnie and Logie Coldstone appear to have been particularly infested with witches. No fewer than fifty-two witch trials seem to have been conducted in 1597 alone, with most of the guilty being put to death. The method of execution included strangulation and burning at the stake, and many a local wise-woman suffered this fate. An allegation that local cows had stopped milking or that a child, formerly healthy, had become sickly was sufficient to point the judicial finger.

The last execution of a Scottish witch took place in Sutherland in 1722, ending what many termed the domination of the devil in local affairs.

2

BRAVEHEARTS

Then came a measure of feudalism – the feudal superiors exploited the locals and built imposing castles at Huntly, Kintore and at Balquhain upon the grabbed land. The Church also made its mark. Abbeys and monasteries were built and the likes of the Abbey of Deer and the Christian foundation at Monymusk came into being.

Royal Burghs followed and in time the Scottish Wars of Independence and those well-documented Jacobite rebellions led the folk of the north-east along a well-trodden path including foreign wars and local insurrection.

Homegrown battles such as those at Alford, Harlaw and Barra set the standard and the likes of the Covenanters and the forces of the unfortunate Marquis of Montrose paid the butcher's bill. However, in the big scheme of things, the civil wars and the bloody victories of the past provide context to today's Aberdeenshire. The farmlands of the north-east contain a multitude of ancient long barrows, stone burial cists, exquisitely carved standing stones and megalithic circles but the jewel in the crown is the proliferation of occasional heroes who somehow made it all possible.

That leads us neatly on to those sometimes famous and those often-unsung heroes – the Bravehearts of the north-east. William Wallace (1270–1305), the brave but nasty Robert the Bruce (1274–1329), and of course that sometimes loved but often reviled reprobate Lord Byron (1788–1824) lead the pack with Mary Webb, George Esson and the quite admirable – one-time prospective Aberdeen City Council candidate – Helena Torry following on not that far behind.

Mind you, the county is literally awash with potential Braveheart candidates. Braemar, for example, boasts a strong connection with Long John Silver of *Treasure Island* fame. Seemingly a consumptive Robert Louis Stevenson penned some dozen chapters of *Treasure Island* during an extended stay in the Highland village. The cottage he reputedly rented now functions as bed and breakfast establishment.

Stonehaven rightly points to solid connections with BBC founding director John Charles Walsham Reith (1889–1971), pneumatic tyre inventor Robert William Thomson (1822–1873) and, of course, communist politician Tom McEwan (1891–1988). Widely known as the 'father of the BBC', Reith's connection with the town is, of course, somewhat tenuous since although the man was born in Evan Street his residency was brief and was somewhat accidental, having taken place midway through a ten-day family holiday at the seaside resort during July 1889. It's a bit like claiming ownership of Donald Trump simply because his mother was born on a Western Isle.

Sandend, population 266, famously boasts a connection with Thomas Blake Glover (1838–1911) – a trader who initiated the formation of the military infrastructure that eventually enabled the Japanese to bomb Pearl Harbor in 1941. And staff at Cruden Bay's Kilmarnock Arms Hotel rightly point visitors to an August 1884 entry in the hotel guest book that reads, 'Delighted with everything and everybody and hope to come again – Mr and Mrs Bram Stoker'.

Infamously, T.E. Lawrence, of Arabia fame, spent a summer in a harbour-side cottage over at Collieston. Well after his Arabian adventures and his later RAF sojourn he had become friendly with a fellow soldier, Jock Bruce from Aberdeen, whom he had met during a brief period of service with the Royal Tank Regiment. Jock was from local farming stock and the adventurous pair apparently shared a healthy interest in sadomasochistic floggings.

A 1984 article in *Leopard Magazine*, co-written by Diane Morgan and David Ross, reveals the pair's craving for sexual gratification via punishment. 'Jock Bruce himself seems to have no qualms about giving Lawrence his scuds,' writes Diane. 'Young and impressionable when they met, he saw himself as Lawrence's bodyguard and valued what he regarded as their friendship – and by no means only for the extra cash it produced.' In her book *Six Buchan Villages*, local author Margaret Aitken relates that the cottage that Lawrence and Bruce inhabited during the hot summer of 1930 was 'a very fine house overlooking the harbour'. Lawrence was less charitable, describing the Collieston cottage as 'the nearest hovel to the high-tide mark.' He also went on record that his fellow flogger, the redoubtable Jock, was 'the roughest diamond in our tank corps hut'.

Aberdeenshire war artist James McBey met Colonel Lawrence during his First World War desert sojourn, and Aberdeen Art Gallery holds a McBey portrait depicting Lawrence in all of his desert finery. Sadly, reproduction of the Lawrence portrait is nowadays subject to a hefty fee and the painting sits hidden deep within the dusty gallery archives. McBey would have been amazed at the absurdity.

Queen Victoria famously spent her holidays at Balmoral, no doubt convinced that empire came a close second to personal happiness. Virtuoso percussionist Dame Evelyn Elizabeth Ann Glennie was born in the county and, of course, that soccer hero and CBE Denis 'The Lawman' Law was born in Aberdeen and at one time lived in a council flat in Printfield Terrace.

The list of Braveheart candidates is endless and even includes *Game of Thrones* heroine Rose Leslie, who grew up within the walls of the splendidly named Lickleyhead Castle just outside Auchleven. But in the big scheme of things, Paisley-born William Wallace and 'King of Scots' Robert the Bruce head the Braveheart pack – not least because both men literally gave their hearts for a cause that they believed in.

William Wallace Statue, Aberdeen (© Duncan Harley)

WILLIAM WALLACE

Robert Burns famously wrote that, 'The story of Wallace poured a Scottish prejudice into my veins which will boil along till the floodgates of time shut in eternal rest', and the citizens of Aberdeen seemingly agreed with this sentiment when, in 1888 or thereabouts, the city fathers erected a statue of the man just opposite His Majesty's Theatre. Bearing an inscription reading, 'I tell you a truth, liberty is the best of all things, my son, never live under any slavish bond', the statue was sculpted by Midlothian sculptor William Grant Stevenson.

Infamously executed by the English in 1305, William Wallace was immortalised by Hollywood when in 1995 the film *Braveheart* starred a kilted Australian actor Mel Gibson as Wallace and took Scotland by storm. Box office success inevitably followed, although the Brigadoon-styled masterpiece soon made British film magazine *Empire*'s list of top ten Worst Best Pictures. Critically reviewed, it was described by Scottish comedy hero Billy Connolly – better known as 'The Big Yin' – as 'A piece of pure Australian crap'.

Despite Connolly's caustic comment, *Braveheart* is held dear by many, although there are perhaps a fair number of Hollywood-scripted historical inaccuracies. Princess Isabella of France, Wallace's sweetheart, for example, is portrayed as being pregnant with the great man's child at the time of his death, despite the fact that history strongly suggests that she did not have her first child until 1312 – a full seven years after the judicial murder. Furthermore, the passionate affair portrayed by Gibson in the film probably never took place since Isabella was born in 1295 and would have been barely 9 years old when Wallace faced his executioners at Smithfield. She probably actually arrived in Britain in February 1308, some five years after her supposed lover's horrific demise. Further bloopers within the 1995 movie include the funeral scene. As the bereaved Wallace bends down to kiss Muron, his murdered bride, a final goodbye, a white delivery van can be seen speeding by just over his left shoulder. The van is travelling very fast and disappears stage-left in a nanosecond, but it's there for all to see. Movie buffs have also spotted continuity issues during one of the battle scenes. Mel Gibson can be seen charging down a hill with a large broadsword in his hand. Moments later he is seen wielding a very small battle-axe before, in a final shot three-quarters of the way down the grassy slope, the large sword reappears in his mighty hand.

In reality, of course, the heroic Wallace did not spend much, if indeed any, of his military career in the north-east, although Aberdeen's twelfth-century St Machar's Cathedral is widely rumoured to be the final resting place of the man's bloodied left arm. His Scottish army, captained probably by a brother, infamously besieged Stonehaven's Dunnottar Castle in 1297 during the Scottish Wars of Independence and is rumoured to have set fire to ships in both Stonehaven and Aberdeen Harbour. In truth William himself probably never visited Aberdeenshire in person, although verse penned by chronicler Blind Harry, writing a century or so after Wallace's death, tells a fanciful tale of his exploits during the siege of Dunnottar Castle:

The Englishmen, that durst them bot abide,
Before the host full fear'dly forth they flee
To Dunnotter, a swake within the sea.
No further they might win out of the land.
They 'sembled there while they were four thousand,
Ran to the kirk, ween'd girth to have tane,
The lave remain'd upon the rock of stane.

The bishop there began to treaty ma,
Their lives to get, out of the land to ga;
But they were rude, and durst not well.
Wallace in fire gart set all hastily,
Burnt up the krik and all that was therein.

Attour the rock the lave ran with great din;
Some hung on crags, right dolefully to dee,
Some lap, some fell, some fluttered in the sea,
No Southern in life was left in that hold.
And them within they burnt to powder cold.
When this was done, feil fell on their knees down,
At the bishop asked absolution.

When Wallace Leugh, said, I forgive you all;
Are ye war-men, repent ye for so small?
They rued not us into the town of Air,
Our true barons when they hanged there!

William Wallace, of course, suffered a much more gruesome fate than those English 'Southern lads'. Following his pivotal role in the Scottish Wars of Independence during the latter part of the thirteenth century he was declared an outlaw by

England's Edward I following defeat at the Battle of Falkirk. Forced to go on the run, he was soon betrayed and then captured by Sir John Menteith near Glasgow on 3 August 1305. Transported to London and sentenced to death by his vengeful captors, the unfortunate hero was dragged in chains behind uncaring horses along the cobbled road to the meat market at Smithfield, and then – while still very much alive – he was hanged slowly by the neck before being stretched on the rack, ritually disembowelled and then castrated. His heart and lungs were then torn out before he was finally and mercifully beheaded. His torso was then hacked into four pieces for distribution around the land as a warning to those who might challenge the power of the king.

A true fate worse than death perhaps. But as Hollywood's distinctly Australian Wallace says in the film version of the Wallace tale: 'We all end up dead, it's just a question of how and why.'

Robert the Bruce under wraps, Aberdeen (© Duncan Harley)

THE BRUCE

A half-size bronze of a mounted King Robert the Bruce, brandishing a replica of the town charter of Aberdeen, sits proudly on Aberdeen's Broad Street just outside the council headquarters at Marischal College. Confusingly inscribed 'Robert the Bruce King of Scots 1306 to 1329' – the Bruce's actual birthdate was 1274, making him much older than 23 when he died – the £120,000 memorial was created by Edinburgh-based sculptor Alan Herriot and funded via the city's Common Good Fund. Some Aberdonians wonder about the merits and demerits of the artwork since the Bruce, in a fit of pique, is widely rumoured to have burned down the town following a good few local skirmishes. In the weeks prior to the official unveiling, the statue stood proudly wrapped in bubble wrap lest the good folk of Aberdeen took umbrage at what some regarded as a misuse of the Common Good Fund.

The death of Alexander III, King of Scots, on the shores of the Firth of Forth in March 1286 had plunged Scotland into a dynastic crisis that was not fully resolved for a further forty years. His neck broken following a fall from his horse, the unlucky Alexander left behind only one direct heir to the Scottish throne – his infant granddaughter, the so-called Maid of Norway. Her death, age 7 in 1290, plunged the country into civil war as the various claimants to the throne vied for supremacy. One such contender was the Bruce.

Crowned at Scone by an obliging sibling, he was soon defeated in battle and driven into hiding by a vengeful English army under Edward I. For a time, he took refuge on Deeside and while he successfully evaded capture – even entering Aberdeen in disguise – his immediate family were not quite so fortunate. Taking refuge at Kildrummy Castle, under the protection of his younger brother Nigel Bruce, his queen and his daughter were betrayed when the castle blacksmith set fire to the castle, forcing the royal family to surrender to the English army. The traitor had been promised a reward of all the gold he could possibly carry and legend insists that the grateful English poured his reward, in the form of a few ladles full of molten gold, down his throat in full and final payment of the debt.

Following a victory to the south at Loudon Hill, Robert the Bruce ventured north, entering Aberdeenshire in the early winter of 1307. On reaching the outskirts of Inverurie he became seriously ill and is said to have spent time recovering at the so-called Bruce's Cave at Ardtannes. Local lore has it that it was here that he met a spider but in reality, caves throughout the land claim ownership of this inspirational tale. Apparently, while recuperating, Bruce watched as the spider tried to construct a web at the cave's entrance. After falling down time and time again the intrepid arthropod finally succeeded, thus inspiring Bruce to take up his mighty sword once again.

Meanwhile, just a few miles to the north, Bruce's enemy – the Earl of Buchan – had encamped outside Oldmeldrum. A skirmish, often called the Battle of Inverurie, took place at a bend on the River Don and shortly after this the still sickly Bruce led his army into battle at the Hill of Barra. His nobles were adamant that he was in no condition to fight but were rebuffed with the response that no medicine could have cured him so quickly as the news that Buchan's troops had attacked Inverurie. 'Either I shall have them, or they shall have me,' he told them. And true to his word he led his army into battle much to the surprise of the enemy, who had imagined him to be still ill and in his sickbed. A splendidly patriotic poem by John Barbour (*c.*1320–1395) records the events:

The king came on in fine array
With much display his foes stood set
Until the ranks were nearly met.
But when his foemen saw the king
Advancing without lingering
A little on their reins they drew.
The king by this time right well knew
That in their hearts they were distressed
And with his banners forward pressed.
Thus, they retreated more and more.
And when the small folk with them saw
Their leaders all retreating so
They quickly turned their backs to go,
And fled and scattered far and wide.
Their lords, that still were side by side,
When they beheld the small folk flee,
And the king advancing steadily,
Themselves became disheartened so
That they, too, turned their backs to go.
A short while stayed they side by side,
And then they scattered far and wide.

The Earl of Buchan's men were, of course, soundly routed at Barra and on Christmas Eve 1307 the defeated remnants of his army were chased as far as Fyvie, where they took refuge within the English-held castle. The royalists made camp at New Deer on the slopes of what is now known as Bruce's Hill. A further battle ensued at Aikey Brae outside Old Deer, after which the defeated Earl of Buchan fled south, allowing Bruce's army free range to plunder the district. There followed a flight to the coast where, with Bruce's mounted soldiers in pursuit, both Buchan and his ally Philip de Mowbray fled south by ship. In what was to become known far and wide as the Harrying of Buchan, Bruce's men set forth to slaughter without mercy anyone loyal to the Earldom of Buchan. Homes, farms and crops were destroyed and livestock slaughtered in a ruthless exercise that was long remembered as an unprecedented campaign of cruelty by fire and sword. An old ballad has it that the Bruce, 'Gert his men burn all Bouchane Fra end to end and sparit nane.'

Following the victory at Barra a portion of Bruce's army entered Aberdeen and, using the password '*Bon Accord*' to distinguish between friend and foe, succeeded in overcoming the local garrison and in burning down Aberdeen Castle. Later, when Bruce granted the town its coat of arms, the motto *Bon Accord* was incorporated in memory of that night attack. As was customary, Robert the Bruce handed out loot in the form of grants of land and titles. Seemingly the citizens of Aberdeen were granted the right to fish the River Dee free of charge, plus the right to hunt in the forests of Stockethill.

The Bruce died in 1329, weakened by ill health and possibly suffering from the ravages of leprosy. His heart was removed and early in 1330 the cardiovascular organ made its way – courtesy of Sir James Douglas, a good friend of the Bruce – towards a final resting place in the far-off Holy Land. Sadly, the silver casket containing the relic only made it as far as Seville, where the unfortunate Douglas was killed by Moorish forces. Bruce's heart then made the journey all the way back to Scotland, where it was placed in perpetuity within Melrose Abbey. His second wife's mortal remains were also to suffer a strange fate.

The church of St Mary in the north-east town of Cullen dates from around 1236 and is situated in what would have been, until the demolition of the old town by an enthusiastic Fifth Earl of Seafield in the 1820s, the very centre of town. Described by archaeologist Ian Shepherd as characteristic of the 'last phase of the medieval church in Scotland with several later additions; the building boasts a fine example of a Lairds Loft dating from 1602 plus both Gothic and Renaissance features', St Mary's was raised to collegiate status in 1543. The building's real claim to fame, however, is as the final resting place of the internal organs of Elizabeth de Burgh. Born at Dunfermline around 1289, she had married Robert the Bruce in 1302 at the age of 13.

After taking refuge in Kildrummy Castle for a period, she fled to Tain following the Bruce's disastrous defeat at the Battle of Methven and was then imprisoned in England for eight years until a prisoner exchange allowed her return to Scotland in 1314.

Elizabeth died at Cullen Castle in 1327 and her entrails were removed for burial in St Mary's Church prior to her embalmed body being taken south to Dunfermline for proper burial. Her husband outlived her by less than two years but is said to have ensured an annual payment be made in perpetuity in gratitude for his wife's kind and respectful treatment by the people of Cullen. Enquiries reveal that no such payment has been recorded in recent centuries and the outstanding bill is said to exceed the entire UK national debt.

In a final twist, royal biographer Andrew Morton has recently revealed that royal bride and American actress Meghan Markle is distantly related to the Scottish hero. Apparently it is possible to trace the bloodline of the Hollywood star of soaps such as *Suits* and *Horrible Bosses* down some twenty-five generations to Robert I of Scotland.

BYRON: MAD, BAD AND DANGEROUS TO KNOW

There's a splendidly spectacular circular hiking route around Gight over at Methlick. Known locally as the Braes of Gight, braes they certainly are. Plunging variously down some 300ft to the River Ythan and back up again, this is not a walk for the faint-hearted and for those more used to the gentle gradients of abandoned railway tracks the walk will fairly take your breath away. Of course, the essence of this trail is its association with the romantic poet, Lord Byron.

'Mad bad and dangerous to know', the poet and adventurer and 6th Baron Byron died in April 1824 aged just 36 years. In a nod to the burial fate of the poet-cum-artist-cum-visionary William Blake (1757–1827), Byron was denied a final resting place amongst his literary equals at Westminster Abbey. Instead, he lies buried alongside the fourteenth-century church of St Mary Magdalene in Hucknall.

Few outside Aberdeenshire realise that he grew up in Aberdeen's Broad Street and spent some more of his youth in the city's Virginia Street before heading off to fame and fortune. Schooled at Aberdeen Grammar, where he apparently carved his initials onto a classroom desk, he has nowadays lent his name to various local businesses including a burger chain and a local recruitment consultancy. A finely chiselled statue of the man clothed in classical attire was unveiled by the Marchioness of Huntly in 1923 and now stands in the grounds of Aberdeen Grammar School. A civic square in Aberdeen's Northfield housing estate is also named in his honour.

With somewhat uninspiring opening lines such as 'O Thou! Who rollest in yon azure field', 'When energising objects men pursue' and 'We do not curse thee, Waterloo!' it's a wonder that anyone reads Byron nowadays, unless forced to by academic requirements. However, despite the flowery verse his work remains popular. He wrote, amongst other works, *Don Juan*. In the classic version of the tale, Don Juan is portrayed as a wealthy Lothario and libertine who devotes his life and soul to the seduction of women. His life is also punctuated with bouts of extreme violence, instances of murder and, inevitably, lots of gambling. The tale's ending depends on which version of the legend one reads.

Tirso de Molina's original play has been interpreted as a religious parable warning against Don Juan's sinful ways and ends with him dying, having been denied salvation by God. Other authors and playwrights have interpreted the ending in their own fashion. Espronceda's Don Felix walks into Hell and to his death of his own volition, while Zorrilla's Don Juan asks for a divine pardon.

Byron's version reverses the classic womanising image of legend, portraying the protagonist not as a womaniser, but as a man easily seduced by women. Written in some 16,000 lines of romantic verse, Byron himself called it an 'epic satire'.

There is much more than mere verse to the romantic poet though. In Greece he was revered for having supported the cause of Greek independence from the Ottoman Empire. In some ways his life of misadventure, if you discount the numerous love affairs and that slightly scandalous incestuous affair with his half-sister, mirrors that of author George Orwell.

Orwell's experiences in the Spanish Civil War might not be too different from those of Byron in the Greek Civil War of Independence. Between 1821 and 1832, Russia, the United Kingdom, France, and several other European powers fought against the Ottoman Empire. Byron was for the Greeks and against the Turks and went so far as to die for the cause in April 1824, aged just 36.

In truth, of course, he died of fever and not from heroic battle wounds, but given his romantic disposition, had he been able to tell of his own demise he would no doubt have immortalised his death in heroic romanticised stanzas.

The good folk of Greece, and in particular the folk of Missolonghi, where Byron met his end, still commemorate his arrival in January 1824 during a lull in the war with Turkey. There are those who to this day feel that had he lived he could have reversed the state of anarchy amongst the Greeks and brought the conflict to a swifter end.

Byron's mother was one Catherine Gordon of Gight. There are, of course, a whole lot of Gordons both in Moray and in Aberdeenshire. Indeed, they are noted as a family who feuded bloodily for centuries. An ancestral Gordon fell at Flodden, another died in Flanders and the survivors of the clan took to murdering each other without mercy over the years, waging war amongst themselves with predictable results. Catherine Gordon of Gight, however, topped the lot in some ways.

Gight Castle is a crumbling ruin nowadays. Set in a place of some beauty and difficult to get to, it was described by Cuthbert Graham in his book *Grampian: The Castle Country* as being associated 'from first to last' with a race

Gight Castle (© Duncan Harley)

whose story was 'crowded with murder and sudden death'. It was George Gordon who built Gight Castle in around 1560. In line with the defensive thinking of the time, it resembled Delgatie Castle in design; measuring around 70ft by 50ft and built on an L-plan, it may even have been commissioned from the same architect. Unlike Delgatie, it has not survived the ravages of the last half millennium.

Catherine Gordon had the misfortune to marry a man known widely as Mad Jack Byron, a conspicuous gambler and sometime Coldstream Guards officer. After Mad Jack had squandered most of her fortune and then deserted her, Catherine took her infant son to Aberdeen, where they lived in rented lodgings on a seemingly meagre income.

Meanwhile, Byron's dad – AKA Mad Foulweather Jack – died in 1791 aged 35 at Valenciennes in Spain. Lord Byron would tell his friends that his father had cut his own throat whilst blind drunk, but that may be an exaggeration. The lands and castle of Gight, however, had to be sold to pay off Mad Jack's gambling debts and the rest is history. The ruin remains a ruin and nowadays cows graze on what might have been Lord Byron's legacy.

Often described as mad, bad and dangerous to know, the Byron surname features in more street names in the UK than many other historic literary figures, according to the Royal Mail. Even Queen Victoria's legacy of street names pales into insignificance when compared to the output of street names commemorating the influential Romantic hero. Apparently, Byron has 608 streets named in his honour and, although he probably never set foot in the city, Birmingham heads the list. When Royal Mail conducted a recent survey to investigate Byron's popularity he outranked both Shelley and Chaucer. Even Wordsworth was found to be wanting with a mere 423 streets recalling his name and, according to Royal Mail, there are just thirteen postcodes in the whole of the UK that ignore the Byron legacy. There is even a pub, The Lord Byron in Aberdeen's Northfield housing estate, named after the man. Now that is an appropriate accolade.

GEORGE ESSON: THE GRAND OLD MAN OF BENNACHIE

In the third edition in the Bennachie Landscapes Series, the historical aspects of the story of Grampian's favourite hill are discussed in minute detail. Dedicated to Gordon Ingram, treasurer to the Bailies of Bennachie until 2000, and with a foreword by Dr Jo Vergunst of the University of Aberdeen's Department of Anthropology, the publication focuses on the ecology and social history of the peak. The geology, the flora and the exploitation of both peat and granite on and around the hill also feature alongside excavation reports featuring the Colony houses and Drumminor Castle.

Several of the Bennachie Landscapes papers make for highly technical reading and are not for the faint hearted. Peter Thorn's description of the geological setting around Drumminor Castle is a case in point. Other chapters such as the interim report into the excavations at Drumminor are written with the general reader in mind and should be accessible to anyone happy to sit through an episode of Sir Tony Robinson's *Time Team*.

The site of the Bennachie Colonists comes under particular scrutiny. Sue Taylor provides insight into the social and domestic lives of the crofters, who made a living on the slopes of the hill, through the interpretation of pottery found at the Bennachie Colony site. The excavations during 2011–13 at Shepherd's Lodge and Hillside yielded both sponge-decorated and transfer-printed earthenware, indicating perhaps a previously unsuspected degree of economic sophistication amongst Colony settlers, who often lived at subsistence level. At its peak the settlement numbered approximately sixty people.

In the twenty-first century, a waymarked path, The Colony Trail, passes through the settlement and the remains of buildings along with traces of long-abandoned kitchen gardens and fields are clearly visible to the casual walker. An anonymous verse on the cover of the Colony Trail Map provides some insight into the life and times of those hardy souls who eked out an existence on the slopes of the hill:

> For the goodly mountain yielded fuel for the fire,
> Stones for the dwelling house, the barn and the byre,
> Heather for roofing and all were gotten free,
> For no oppressive landlord could swallow Bennachie.

So, who were those so-called Bennachie Colonists? Well, an obituary in the local Inverurie paper, dated 3 June 1939, holds something of a clue. Described as the grand old man of Bennachie, George Esson had passed away in his 76th year. He died at his croft at Boghead, Tullos, a place described as 'a humble sheiling surrounded by a croft of 6–8 acres which his forefathers had reclaimed from the heather and the wasteland of the hill'.

George Esson (Courtesy of the Bailies of Bennachie)

George came from a family of squatters who had settled on the land at the base of the hill many years before. The cottager's life was by all accounts hard and the oft repeated description 'three acres and a cow' provides something of a clue to the hardships of upland crofting life.

To supplement the lifestyle, George had worked as a dry stane dyker and from a young age he plied his trade amongst the local farming community. Much of his handiwork can be seen around the district to this day, albeit repaired or in modern-day ruin. The dykes on the Pittodrie Estate and at Dunecht bear silent witness to his skill.

George Esson's obituary goes on to describe the misfortune which, 'A good many years ago befell the squatters on Bennachie.' They had, it seems, been sitting rent-free by virtue of the fact that they had reclaimed the heather-strewn land and built themselves houses, but by order of the Court of Session in Edinburgh and at the behest of the local landed gentry, they had been legally, and some might say scandalously, evicted.

A 'wave of indignation' swept the county when the evictions began. But with the backing of the law, most of the so-called Bennachie Colonists were forced off the land they had occupied for decades and finally George's family alone remained.

Some years later George's wee croft was put on sale at the behest of the laird of Fetternear Estate but George refused to put up the nominal figure asked by the now benevolent laird. The landowner, a Mr Anderson of Fingask, then offered George his croft at a peppercorn rent, although it seems likely that the rent was never actually collected.

George's great hobby was bees and he kept between thirty and forty hives on the slopes of Bennachie. On his death a roup was held to sell off his tools and possessions and a neighbour, a Mrs Smith from Blairdaff, purchased his bee skeps along with his collection of gramophone records.

The obituary piece in the local Garioch newspaper records that George was possibly the last of his race. His wife, Mary Ann Knight, had predeceased him and there were no children. The article records that 'with the passing of George, the Garioch has lost a personality'.

Apparently he published a now out of print book on the local history of the Garioch. The newspaper obituary concludes that George, 'In appearance, was about as rough as his native Bennachie, but he had a kindly and warm heart.' On his headstone are the words: 'George Esson – Descended from the first and himself the last of the colonists of Bennachie'.

A MERRY DANCER

Aptly described by north-east author and journalist Jack Webster as that 'Anthem of Aberdonianism', the song 'The Northern Lights of Old Aberdeen' is known throughout the world and is indelibly associated with the Granite City:

The northern lights of old Aberdeen
Mean home sweet home to me
The northern lights of Aberdeen
Are what I long to see
I've been a wanderer all of my life
And many a sight I've seen
God speed the day, when I'm on my way
To my home in Aberdeen.

When I was a lad, a tiny wee lad
My mother said to me
Come see the northern lights my boy
They're bright as they can be
She called them the heavenly dancers
Merry dancers in the sky
I'll never forget that wonderful sight
They made the heavens bright.

I've wandered in many far off lands
And travelled many a mile
I've missed the folk I've cherished the most
The joy of a friendly smile
It warms up the heart of the wanderer
The clasp of a welcoming hand
To greet me when I return
Home to my native land.

The northern lights referred to in the lyrics refer to the Heavenly Dancers, sometimes known as the Merry Dancers, which brighten up the skies during periods of intense solar activity. Although predominantly seen in the high-latitude regions around the Arctic, the trademark red and green curtains of light of the Aurora Borealis are visible in the night sky from most points of the north-east as and when atmospheric conditions permit and where light pollution is at a minimum. So how did this heart-warmingly patriotic song come to be associated with Aberdeen? Well, a battered old upright piano now in the care of Aberdeen City Council holds the clue to the tale.

When the Victorian era Aberdeen Music Hall closed for much-needed renovations in 2016, a series of public events was organised during the weeks leading up to the closure. Titled 'Lights Oot!' the final performances showcased the diversity of the venue and celebrated the entertainments that had drawn the folk of Aberdeen and Aberdeenshire to the hallowed place over the years. Built to a design by architect Archibald Simpson, the building opened in 1822, initially as a private membership-only gentleman's club, and over the intervening decades performers as diverse as Charles Dickens, John Anderson the Great Wizard of the North, plus the comedy string-puppet duo Pinky and Perky have trodden the boards to both entertain and amaze local audiences. Politicians Tony Benn, Sir Winston Churchill and Lloyd George put in appearances and throughout its history the building has played host to everything from concerts and bazaars to theatre and sporting events. Rocket-Man Elton John can still remember playing his first ever Aberdeen gig at the venue in 1972 and many Aberdonians can recall their shock introduction to Glam Rock a year later when David Bowie plus legendary guitarist Mick Ronson brought the Spiders from Mars to the Music Hall stage. When, in 1993, the city's Lord Provost welcomed Mikhail Gorbachev – a much-needed riposte to the misery of post-war Soviet life – to Aberdeen to receive the Freedom of the City, the Music Hall was the venue of choice for the civic reception. And in the days when Aberdeen boasted a repertory theatre, around 1949, the Aberdeen Repertory Theatre regularly performed on the historic boards of the Ballroom Stage.

The March 2016 closure week saw a performance of Aidan O'Rourke and Jason Singh's experimental sound work 'Connect:ed' [*sic*]. The very next night the Music Hall hosted a final production titled 'Your Hall, Your Story'. Following an introductory speech from Aberdeen Provost George Adams, the evening focused on the recollections and reminiscences of the users of the venue. Compere Robert Lovie and actor Cameron Mowat led the audience of around 600 on a journey through the sometimes turbulent but always entertaining history of Aberdeen's favourite concert venue using both live and recorded recollections told first-hand by those who were actually there. The stories came fast and furious throughout the evening. Roberta Duncan told how her father rose to international fame following a world record roller-skating endurance marathon in the main hall. His record-making 61-hour stint seemingly stands to this day. Mary Smith remembered meeting Sir John Barbirolli at a Hallé Orchestra performance, Aberdonian Sandy Hood recalled listening to Mahler at the venue and a local councillor, former European and Commonwealth lightweight wrestler Len Ironside, told how fellow wrestlers had a particular dislike of the Music Hall wrestling ring. 'It was up on stage,' he said, 'which meant that you felt every bump and had every chance of being thrown out of the ring and down the ten feet or so to the floor. When this happened, the audience would simply lift you up and throw you back in.' On one occasion he recalled that as this was going on, a voice rang out, 'Is there any word yet aboot' ma new hoose please councillor Ironside?'

Strangely perhaps, although 'The Northern Lights of Old Aberdeen' song did feature in the 'Lights Oot!' performances, Mary Webb's battered old John Broadwood piano, sitting just a few dozen yards from the historic Music Hall stage in the Mary Garden room, failed to put in an appearance. Perhaps the promoters of the 'Lights Oot!' event had been unaware that the Broadwood was probably the very one that English concert pianist Mary Webb, the composer of the tune, had used to write the once-heard-never-forgotten classic that symbolises Aberdonianism the world over.

Leamington Spa-born Mary was funding her musical career by working as a food-prep operative in the kitchens of the West London Hospital alongside a homesick Aberdeen lass by the name of Winnie Forgie. A friendship developed between the two and, in an effort to cheer up the lonely Aberdonian, Mary and her husband co-wrote the tune and the lyrics. Eventually she sent these off to Scottish tenor Robert Wilson, who performed the piece during a concert at the Royal Albert Hall. As a result, the iconic song became well known across the globe.

Mary Webb's piano (© Duncan Harley)

In 1958, some six years after composing the song, Mary was invited to Aberdeen – a place she had never previously visited – where she performed at the city's Victorian era Tivoli Theatre, having been coaxed onstage from amongst the audience by none other than Robert Wilson. The standing ovation she received that night, however, did not lead to wealth and riches and decades later, in 1989, Mary Webb died alone, largely forgotten and in desperate poverty at London's Charing Cross Hospital aged 82. Thanks largely to the intervention of Jack Webster, her piano was gifted to Aberdeen City Council and until the Music Hall closure the instrument sat seemingly forgotten at the venue with little apart from an A4 poster to mark the fact that the battered relic was instrumental in the heritage of the city of Aberdeen.

As a postscript, Mary was cremated at Oakley Wood Crematorium near Leamington during what Jack Webster recalls as 'a brief and pathetic finale; few even in her own native area having the slightest idea of her significance'. He goes on to write that, following the service, both her ashes and her piano were made available and in due course both made their way north to Aberdeen where, during a more respectful remembrance service on 23 August 1989, Mary Webb's ashes were scattered within the grounds of Kaimhill Crematorium at Garthdee.

HELENA TORRY: THE VOICE OF THE SILENT MAJORITY

In April 2012 newspapers up and down the country reported on the strange case of a political activist by the name of Helena Torry. The hustings for the local council elections were under way and Helena had announced that she was standing for Aberdeen's Hazlehead, Ashley and Queens Cross ward as 'the voice of the silent majority'.

Helena's campaign agent Renée Slater duly filed the required official nomination papers with the city council returning officer and all seemed well until the afternoon of 2 April, when the council issued an Amended Notice of Poll for the ward along with a statement from returning officer Valerie Watts stating that, 'It has been brought to my attention that Helena Torry, for whom a nomination paper was submitted for the Hazlehead, Ashley and Queens Cross Ward, does not exist!' Heads were seemingly about to roll.

It quickly became obvious that the authorities in charge of the nomination process were not at all pleased and in due course Helena's campaign agent, Torry resident and political activist Renee Slater, was visited by police and charged under Section 65, part 2A of the Representation of the People Act 1983 with the felony of forging official nomination papers. But of course, the vivacious Helena did in fact exist and, although she proved to be a humble shop window mannequin, her voice of protest was soon being heard across the international airwaves and indeed the front pages of many UK and foreign newspapers. Headlines screamed 'Cops Seize Election Dummy', 'Dummy Runs' and 'Free Helena Torry'.

A Sheriff Court appearance ensued, during which Ms Slater's legal representative, Gregor Kelly of Lefevre Litigation, informed the court that Renée had 'told the police that she sought to inject humour into an austere process' and 'did not seek to belittle or demean the electoral process'. Renee, who faced up to six months in prison, was quickly found not guilty following a submission by the defence that the Crown had not produced any evidence of impropriety and therefore there was no case to answer. Sheriff Hammond agreed and Renee walked free from court commenting, 'It's brilliant, I never felt that I was guilty, it was all about local authority cutbacks. There's no voice for those affected and I simply thought, let's give the silent majority a voice ... Helena had personality without opening her mouth ... she had more charisma than the politicians.'

Renée Slater was free but the council candidate was destined to remain in police custody for the next few months within a locked cupboard at Aberdeen police headquarters.

Helena Torry (© Margaret Maclean)

Interviewed on the Andrew Neil *Daily Politics* show, Renée revealed that she herself had in fact spent time in custody after being charged. 'I was in a police cell for around six hours and they wouldn't let me out until I handed in Helena. It was a sort of prisoner exchange.' Andrew Neil asked, 'Is the mannequin still in jail and has she been mistreated?' to which Renee replied that she thought that Helena might be let out very soon: 'I think she might need a change of clothes by now though.'

'I hope she's not been waterboarded in the meantime,' retorted the well-seasoned BBC presenter.

The case of Helena Torry is not unique. In fact, there is a long history of lampooning in parliamentary elections, although the term 'dummy candidate' is usually reserved for would-be politicians who enter the race with the sole intention of ruining the opposition's chances of election. David Edward Sutch, the self-ennobled 3rd Earl of Harrow, also known as Screaming Lord Sutch, was a case in point. A fixture on the political scene for several decades he often lost his deposit but on occasion upstaged even Prime Ministers. Mind you, he was no Aberdonian shop window mannequin and he infamously stood as the Official Monster Raving Loony Party candidate. Perhaps in the not too distant future Helena Torry will be back on the campaign trail again.

3

BLOODY BATTLES

The north-east of Scotland has witnessed many battles over the various eons, although some, such as the Battle of Inverurie, might perhaps be better defined as simply a minor skirmish. The Battle of Inverurie – not to be confused with Bruce's campaign of 1308 or indeed those twentieth-century battles between the youth of Kemnay and those of Oldmeldrum at Meldrum Sports – took place in December 1745 when a small force of Royalists was attacked by some 900 Jacobites led by a contingent of French mercenaries at the southern end of the town. After a short running fight in the streets of the town, the Royalists dispersed and the Jacobites gained control of most of Aberdeenshire.

In their turn Lumphanan, Aberdeen, Fyvie and Alford were to be the scene of fierce fighting at various points in the county's history. Viking raids and murderous blood feuds added stirring tales of derring-do to the mix. Perhaps surprisingly, however, the 1411 Battle of Harlaw has emerged as one of the better-known skirmishes in the history of the area. Despite the wildly differing accounts of the bloodletting and the oddly skewed politics that prevented the memorial to the event being fully completed for some 100 years, the Battle of Harlaw remains in popular imagination a victory by the good citizens of Aberdeen over the kilted savages of Donald, Lord of the Isles. Nothing could be further from the truth, since not only did Donald have a degree of legitimacy in his claim to the Earldom of Ross but, in truth, the numbers of Aberdonians present on the day were probably in the low hundreds. Be that as it may, Reid Harlaw, or Bloody Harlaw, remains an important event and the good and the great of the Granite City have long claimed ownership of the victory.

BLOODY HARLAW

A special train left the Joint Station at Aberdeen on Friday, 24 July 1914 and headed north to the old railway station at Inverurie, where it stopped to pick up a number of very important passengers before proceeding to a point midway between Inverurie and Inveramsay. Wooden ladders were lowered onto the track and, on that damp and blustery pre-First World War summer's day, some 300 passengers disembarked then trudged up through the muddy fields to join crowds of locals who had gathered to witness the inaugural ceremony of the monument to the July 1411 Battle of Harlaw.

The battle is often portrayed as a simple bloodthirsty clash between Highland and Lowland cultures, and popular belief holds that the outcome saved the city of Aberdeen from rape and pillage at the hands of the highland hordes. The Lord of the Isles was indeed a troublesome noble. He looked upon himself as legitimate heir to the Earldom of Ross and when the Duke of Albany, who had become Regent following the death of King Robert III, refused to grant the claim – giving it to his own son – Donald gathered an army and invaded the disputed territory. Some historians, however, wonder why this is so well remembered. It was, after all, a fairly minor clash despite the appalling loss of life. And, in the big scheme, the clash of arms between the warring factions achieved little. Post-battle, both sides retreated to lick their wounds and, as always, the common soldier, the camp followers and the ladies of the baggage train paid the bloody price.

Donald's plan had been to give his battle-hardened but cash-hungry army a shot at some well-earned booty and, of course, he hoped to expand his territory in a further land-grab. His regiments, numbering perhaps as many as 10,000 men-at-arms plus a further few thousand camp-followers, entered the rich farmlands of the Garioch through the Glens of Foudland and made their way south on foot past Culsamond, Insch and Old Rayne before coming to a dead stop at Harlaw in the face of determined opposition organised by the Earl of Mar. Son of the infamous Wolf of Badenoch of cathedral-burning fame, Mar had foreseen the Highland danger well in advance and had summoned men from as far south as Dundee to counter the threat. Local knights including Sir Alexander Irvine of Drum, Sir Andrew Leslie of Balquhain and Sir Henry Preston of Fyvie rallied to the cause, as did a contingent from Aberdeen under the command of Lord Provost Robert Davidson.

Donald of the Isles commanded the heights and Mar's force, numbering perhaps 2,500, had the difficult task of charging up the long grassy slope towards what is nowadays known as Balhaggardy. The hand-to-hand conflict ebbed and flowed until near dawn the next day with successive onslaughts being fiercely repulsed and with no obvious victory for either army. Finally, both sides fought each other to a complete standstill. Much of the action of that day is recalled in somewhat heroic ballad form:

As I came in by Dunnideer and down by Netherha.
There were fifty thousand Hielanmen all marching to Harlaw.
As I came on, and farther on, and down and by Balquhain,
Oh there I met Sir James the Rose, wi him Sir John the Gryme.

'Oh, came ye frae the Hielans man? An came ye a' the way?
Saw ye Macdonell and his men as they came frae the Skye?'
'Yes, me cam frae ta Hielans, man, an me cam a' ta wye,
An she saw Macdonell his men, as they cane frae ta Skye.'

'Oh was ye near Macdonell's men? Did ye their numbers see?
Come, tell to me, John Hielanman, what micht their numbers be?'
'Yes, me was near, an near eneuch, an me their numbers saw;
There was fifty thousand Hielanmen a marching to Harlaw.'

Gin that be true,' says James the Rose, we'll no come meikle speed;
'We'll cry upon our merry men and lichtly mount our steed.
Oh no, oh no,' says John the Gryme. 'That thing maun never be;
The gallant Grymes were never bate, we'll try what we can dee.

As I came on, an farther on, an doun and by Harlaw,
They fell fu close on ilka side; Sic fun ye never saw.
They fell fu close on ilka side, sic fun ye never saw;
For Hielan swords gied clash for clash, at the battle o Harlaw.

The Hielanmen, wi their lang swords, they laid on us fu sair,
An they drave back our merry men three acres breadth an mair.
Brave Forbes to his brither did say, noo brither, dinna ye see?
They beat us back on ilka side, an we'll be forced to flee.
Oh no, oh no, my brither dear, that thing maun never be;
Tak ye your good sword in your hand, an come your wa's wi me.
Oh no, oh no, my brither dear, the clans they are ower strang,
An they drive back our merry men wi swords baith sharp an lang.

Brave Forbes drew his men aside, said, Tak your rest a while,
Until I to Drumminnor send, to fess my coat o mail.
The servant he did ride, an his horse it did na fail,
For in twa hours an a quarter he brocht the coat o mail.

Then back to back the brithers twa gaed in among the thrang,
An they hewed doun the Heilanmen, wi swords baith sharp an lang.
Macdonell, he was young an stout, had on his coat o mail,
An he has gane oot throw them a, to try his han' himsell.

The first ae straik that Forbes strack, he garrt Macdonell reel,
An the neist ae straik that Forbes strack, the great Macdonell fell.

An siccan a lierachie I'm sure ye never saw
As wis amo the Hielanmen, when they saw Macdonell fa.

An whan they saw that he was deid, they turnd an ran awa,
An they buried him in Leggett's Den, a large mile frae Harlaw.
They rade, they ran, an some did gang, they were o sma record;
But Forbes an a his merry men, they slew them a' the road.

On Monanday, at mornin, the battle it began,
On Saturday, at gloamin, ye'd scarce kent wha had wan.
An sic a weary buryn I'm sure ye never saw
As wis the Sunday after that, on the muirs aneath Harlaw.

Gin ony body speer at you for them ye took awa,
Ye may tell their wives and bairnies;
They're sleeping at Harlaw.

Following the slaughter, the Highlanders melted away to the north and the power of the Lord of the Isles was so weakened that in 1412 he was forced to submit to the Scottish Crown. Aberdeen City and Aberdeenshire were spared the wrath of Highland domination but, of course, many combatants, some famous, lay dead and dying on the battlefield. The city's Provost Davidson was slain and his body returned to Aberdeen for burial in Collison's Aisle within St Nicholas Church, and one local laird, Sir Andrew Leslie of Balquhain, lost all six of his sons. Provost Davidson remains the only serving Aberdeen lord provost, to date, to have suffered death on the field of battle.

THE HARLAW MONUMENT

For several hundred years the battlefield lacked a decent monument. There were sites identified in the locality that were rumoured to house the mass graves of the dead. The

The Harlaw Monument (© Duncan Harley)

Liggart Stone is said to mark the final resting place of camp-followers murdered in the post-battle bloodletting. Another, now lost, mass grave may have contained captives executed in the aftermath. Over at nearby Kinkell graveyard the ornate tomb of Gilbert de Greenlaw, a knight who fought and perished on the field at Harlaw, languishes within a ruined church.

In 1911 Professor Davidson of the University of Aberdeen, a descendant of the fallen Provost Davidson, suggested that the Aberdeen City Council should commemorate the 500th anniversary of the battle. A sub-committee of the City Finance Committee visited the battlefield for a recce and agreed to release funding. As a result, the tall granite memorial we see today was commissioned.

Constructed of Corennie granite at a cost of £350 and standing some 45ft high, the monument was designed by Aberdeen architect William Kelly of Kelly's Cats fame and is sited near the spot where Provost Davidson is said to have fallen. Puzzlingly, the monument for many years remained incomplete. About 16ft from the ground Kelly had made provision for the placement of several armorial plaques bearing the coats of arms of the principal combatants on both sides.

A letter published in the February 2010 issue of *Leopard Magazine* gives a clue to the mystery of the missing armorial shields. In the letter, Ross Herald of Arms, Charles Burnett reveals that as 'three of the arms were to represent Macdonald, Maclean and Macintosh, there was an objection to paying for the arms of the "enemy" and as a result no heraldry was added to the monument'. The Ross Herald of Arms goes on to say that the arms 'originally to be included were: City of Aberdeen, Leslie, Mar, Forbes, Irvine, Keith, Leith, Ogilvy, Scrymgeour, Macdonald, Maclean and Macintosh'.

Finally, in 2011, when passions had cooled, the missing shields were added to the Harlaw Monument in time for the 600th anniversary of what had become known locally as 'Reid Harlaw'.

In a further twist, the booklet recording the order of events for the inaugural ceremony that took place in 1914 records that among the 300 invited guests, there was a contingent of German naval officers in dress uniform. Following a loyal toast to the King, Lord Provost Maitland proposed a toast to the German Kaiser. Following suitable applause Commander Sebelin, the most senior German officer present, replied, 'I think it a very great honour that you recognise our Emperor on this occasion.'

Just a few weeks later, on 4 August 1914, Britain would be at war with Germany. Commander Sebelin went on to sink thirteen Allied ships during the conflict. He died when his submarine, the UC43, was sunk with all hands by the Royal Navy in the North Sea on 10 March 1917.

The Monymusk Reliquary

THE MONYMUSK RELIQUARY

In August 2014 Edinburgh Auctioneers Lyon & Turnbull offered for sale a small decorative wooden box believed to be the work of Alexander J. Brook of Edinburgh silversmiths Brook & Sons. Brook was known for his meticulously researched reproductions of antiquarian items and the small (width: 112mm x diameter: 51mm x height: 89mm) highly decorated, silver-plated wooden casket would have presented few challenges for him.

Brook's nineteenth-century replica was of an item known as the Monymusk Reliquary. The unsigned piece had been valued at between £5,000 and £10,000; however, perhaps due to interest in all things Scottish generated during the run-up to the Scottish Referendum and the approaching 700th anniversary of the Battle of Bannockburn, the tiny, silver panelled, yew wood container fetched a staggering £20,000 on sale day.

A strange prequel to the sale had been played out some seventy-nine years before, in 1933, when the original Monymusk Reliquary had been advertised for sale by auction in a London saleroom.

According to National Museums Scotland, who now hold the circa eighth-century reliquary in their permanent collection, 'Portable reliquaries were carried on campaign with the Scottish army' and the Monymusk Reliquary 'is thought to have been the so-called Brechbennoch of St Columba which was with the army at the Battle of Bannockburn in 1314'. Widely supposed to have once contained a holy relic of St Columba, the Brechbennoch, was regarded as a sort of good luck charm on the battlefield and was carried – probably on a leather halter around the neck of its keeper – at the head of the Scottish army as a sacred battle ensign. The tale of how the reliquary came into the care of National Museums Scotland is a strange one.

King William the Lion had founded the great abbey at Arbroath partly in memory of Thomas à Becket, a friend since childhood, who had been murdered in 1170 while praying within Canterbury Cathedral. Among the gifts bestowed by the king at the time of the establishment of the abbey were Church lands at Forglen just outside Turriff. Along with the lands came the Brechbennoch and, although there is mystery regarding its earlier history, King William made a point of gifting the precious object to the abbey along with an obligation that it should be carried into battle ahead of the Scottish army by the guardians of the abbey. In 1315, some seven months after Bernard de Linton, the abbot at Arbroath, had carried the reliquary into battle at Bannockburn, he passed on the somewhat dangerous responsibility to Malcolm of Monymusk, along with the lands at Forglen as a sweetener in the deal. The reliquary seems to have moved back to Aberdeenshire along with the Forglen title deeds and there it remained until 1933, when the precious relic turned up in that London auction house.

In the meantime, it is widely supposed to have resided at the Monymusk Priory until a disastrous fire in 1554 resulted in its removal to nearby Monymusk House. Latterly Monymusk House was the domain of the Grants and a concerned Scottish nation was mobilised both by the press of the day but also by the efforts of the then head of the National Museum of Antiquities of Scotland, Graham Callander, who took the view that the Brechbennoch of St Columba rightly belonged to the Scottish nation. Callander, aided by a group of influential friends, took in hand the task of raising the necessary money to purchase the relic and politicians such as Prime Minister Sir Ramsay MacDonald became involved. Even the Queen became interested in the affair and she was rumoured to have visited the saleroom. After furious debate, both in the press and in parliament, as to the right of the Laird at Monymusk to sell the much-venerated relic, the item was withdrawn from the sale and following an agreement with the heir to the estate it was acquired by the National Museum of Antiquities of Scotland, where it remains to this day.

4

AGRICULTURAL IMPROVEMENTS

The various Statistical Accounts of Scotland offer rich pickings to the budding historian. Essentially a series of documentary publications related in subject matter though published at different times, they cover life in Scotland in the eighteenth, nineteenth and twentieth centuries. Those needing to know how many acres of land were under cultivation in any shire in Scotland in 1791 need look no further. And those who seek to understand the lot of the ordinary folk of past times will not be disappointed. Since the accounts were often commissioned from the local clergy, alongside the counting of sheep and the estimation of the acres in cultivation an element of judgemental prose often haunts the tomes. In an account of Inverurie, for example, we learn that the population are generally sober and industrious; this despite the eighteen or so public houses that then served hard liquor to the thirsty townsfolk.

The Old Statistical Account of Scotland was published between 1791 and 1799 by Sir John Sinclair while later volumes were published under the auspices of the General Assembly of the Church of Scotland between 1834 and 1845. These two early series are held by some to be among the finest European contemporary records of life in the towns and countryside of Scotland during the Agricultural Revolution. Other publications such as Alexander Mackie's

1911 classic *Aberdeenshire* mimicked the early accounts and described the county of Aberdeenshire in cold statistical terms.

Thus we learn from Mackie's account that in the pre-Turnip Townshend era 'as many as 12,000 beef cattle' were annually sent to England via droving routes, the remainder being killed and salted at the end of the season since there was insufficient winter feed to tide the beasts over. The advent of steam navigation, he writes, put paid to this annual migration and the drovers were soon vying with both the steam trains and the coastal steamships for trade. By 1909, he records that there were an astonishing 204,490 agricultural horses in the entirety of Scotland, of which 31,592 were to be found in Aberdeenshire. There were also 168,091 cattle and the county could boast almost a quarter of a million sheep – second only to the County of Argyll, which topped the polls at nearly a million.

The introduction of new and improved farming methods fuelled this period of change and while it was the farmers, often tenanted, who did most of the hard work it was the landowners who often pointed the way. Sir Archibald Grant of Monymusk and Alexander Udny of Udny were early pioneers of better practices and many a boulder-strewn wilderness gave way to riches beyond anyone's anticipation. An early improver, Sir Archibald Grant (1696–1778), devoted his life to transforming his estate at Monymusk from a medieval style of penury to an enlightened modernism. He introduced the humble neep as a field crop, drained the boggy fields around his estate and built dykes and roads using stones taken off the improved fields. He is reputed to have planted several million trees during his lifetime and remnants of his enlightened forestry can be seen today at Paradise Wood near the Grant ancestral home.

Sir Archibald's reforms were, he said, inspired by his 'very worthy father' and he writes that, 'I was allowed in 1716, although then very young, to begin to enclose and plant and provide and prepare nurseries.' Seemingly, 'At that time there was not one acre upon the whole estate enclosed, nor any timber upon it but a few elms, sycamore and ash about a small kitchen garden adjoining to the house, and some straggling trees at some of the farm yards, with a small copse wood, not enclosed and dwarfish and browsed by sheep and cattle.' Archibald was soon to change all of that, and for the better.

Before his ascendance, the accepted farming practice in Aberdeenshire, and indeed across much of Scotland, was the old and detrimental infield and outfield system. The infield was never rested and grew constant crops often stunted through lack of nutrients; while the outfield was used for several years before being left fallow then put back into cultivation. Crop yields were subsequently poor and agricultural inputs, aside from the casual droppings of sheep and cattle, were largely neglected. It was almost as though folk imagined that, as if by some Mother Earth magic, the land would somehow regenerate given sufficient time. And indeed, until the coming of the canal and the railway, the Shire was destined to suffer from a poverty of the soil.

Fortunately, Sir Archibald obtained a copy of Jethro Tull's bestseller *Horse Hoeing and Animal Husbandry* for the then equivalent of 50p, and began revolutionising the farming practices of the county. Clover was sown and then ploughed back in to enrich the depleted soil, a rotation of crops was introduced and modern ploughs were imported from England – the oxen-drawn Scotch ploughs of the day were heavy, unwieldy and often inefficient. By the mid-1700s the improved farming practices had transformed the Monymusk estate beyond all recognition.

The notions of crop rotation, fallowing and winter feed-crops had been learned and oats, clover, rye, wheat, cabbage, turnips, barley, potatoes and even lint were in regular production. Sir Archibald's Monymusk estate was well ahead of the game as far as the farming practices of the time were concerned and the consequent wealth in the form of the planned village of Monymusk and the laird's grand house down by the banks of the River Don are testament to his foresight. By the summer of 1752 his estate boasted some thirty-seven horses and 263 oxen, and the lands at Monymusk had at last become an important source of income for both tenant farmer and landowner.

Alongside the farming, the improvements and the forestry, Sir Archibald was married four times during his long and busy life. Outlived by his fourth wife, he died in 1778 and although ownership of slave plantations in far off Jamaica were to taint the family reputation in later years, the Aberdeenshire Grants are generally held in high regard even to this day.

THE BLENHEIM OF BUCHAN

A clear example of the accumulation of wealth through agricultural improvement can be seen at Old Deer, where remnants of the grand old estate of Pitfour remain in evidence. At one time, the estate of Pitfour was one of the largest and arguably one of the grandest estates in the north-east of Scotland. Between 1700 and 1924, the six incumbent lairds of Pitfour variously improved, enjoyed and finally depleted the capital of the estate known affectionately as 'The Blenheim of Buchan' – a reference to the richly landscaped Oxfordshire estate of the Dukes of Marlborough.

At its peak, Pitfour controlled around 30,000 acres of the Buchan countryside. Amid the grandeur stood the fifty-two-roomed Pitfour House, the quite extraordinary Temple of Theseus – a scaled down replica of the Athenic Temple of Hephaestus replete with an aquarium in which George, the 5th laird, was believed to have kept alligators – plus a private racecourse with stables, a chapel and even a riding school that doubled as a ballroom for large social events. Long, tree-lined drives, decorative fountains and sunken gardens completed the spectacular visitor experience. Pitfour House is long gone, although many historic structures, including the Greek temple and the stables, survive, albeit some in poor condition.

Nowadays, Pitfour Estate's most obviously intact historic building is Saplinbrae. Built in around 1766 and extended in about 1850 using plundered stone from nearby Deer Abbey, the building has had several incarnations. Nowadays operating as a hotel, it once served as a manse before becoming a dower house for the use of the 5th laird's mother-in-law. In the early twentieth century, Saplinbrae became home to the 6th and last laird of Pitfour, James Ferguson – the Great Improver.

THE GREAT IMPROVERS

The first three Ferguson lairds of Pitfour can be fairly credited with growing and improving the estate. The 4th laird had little time to make any changes or indeed any improvements. He was in fact laird only for a few months before his death, in December 1820, at age 72. The decline in the estate's fortunes can be laid firmly at the door of the 5th and 6th lairds, who freely spent the family fortune and eroded the estate's capital to the point of eventual bankruptcy.

Perhaps the greatest improver of Pitfour was James Ferguson – the 3rd laird. Alongside running the estate, he served as MP, first for Banffshire and then for Aberdeenshire, and was laird from 1777 to 1820. Popular lore holds that he spoke only once in Parliamentary debate, when he moved that a draughty window behind his seat in the Commons chamber be mended. His unexpected speech led to cries of 'Hear hear!' from those present, whereupon James is said to have paused for a moment before replying, 'I'll be damned if you do,' after which he sat down, never to speak publicly in the House again.

In the early years of the nineteenth century, James indulged his favourite sport of angling. Inspired by the Prince Regent's Lake at Windsor, a valley between two streams on the Pitfour estate was deepened and dammed. The result was the 40-acre Pitfour Lake we see today. The new lake was stocked with trout, tench and perch, and a cable-drawn passenger ferry was installed at the westward end to link Pitfour House with the Temple of Theseus. A colony of imported swans completed the idyllic scene.

Despite his possibly sparse Parliamentary speaking record, James must have been influential both locally and at Westminster. He is credited with substantially upgrading the Buchan road system and the improved road between Banff and Peterhead was seemingly constructed under his auspices. It has often been claimed that Pitfour's decline was due to James's ambitious scheme to cut a canal from Pitfour to the sea, at Peterhead.

Canal building in Scotland was popular around 1800. The Forth and Clyde Canal had opened in 1790 and the Inverurie to Aberdeen canal had been completed in 1805. James's canal was on a much more modest scale and projected costs were a mere £4,000 – a sum unlikely to cause the wealthy laird sleepless nights. Digging began around 1797, but by 1800, work had virtually ceased. Forces of nature, in the form of the need to divert river water to top-up the canal, had combined with the forces of commerce, in the form of litigation by local mill owners fearful of the depletion of their vital water supplies, and the project was never completed. Some remnants of the Buchan Canal can still be seen near St Fergus.

GEORGE FERGUSON: THE GREAT SPENDER

If James Ferguson, the 3rd laird of Pitfour, was the great improver, then George Ferguson, 5th laird of Pitfour and illegitimate son of the 4th laird – also a George – was undoubtedly the great spender. His father, despite being in possession of the estate for only a few months prior to his death in 1820, had added considerable revenue to the family coffers through his ownership of slave plantations in Tobago.

Known as 'The Admiral' because of his naval background, the 5th laird was already heavily in debt when he took over the reins. Estimates vary, however, it is likely that the family fortune he inherited exceeded £300,000. He was to run Pitfour from 1821 until his death in 1867. Born in 1788 and educated for a career in the navy, he embarked as a midshipman on the thirty-eight-gun frigate HMS *Hussar*, in 1800. He saw his first active service in 1804, while serving on a British warship engaged in raiding seaports and coastal batteries along the French coast. The threat of French invasion hung over the UK and the British navy was fully engaged in asserting its supremacy over the French. In 1804, the laird found himself in action against a French privateer, the thirty-gunned *Blonde*, which surrendered and thus became a prize after a running fight.

In 1805, aged almost 17, George was promoted to lieutenant and by age 21 had gained his first independent command, in charge of the eighteen-gun sloop HMS *Pylades*. It was in this ship that George came to the notice of the Lords of the Admiralty when, during a November storm, he sighted an abandoned timber carrier, the London-registered sailing ship *Hebe*, drifting and waterlogged off the Aberdeenshire coast. Having towed his prize into Peterhead Harbour he took the opportunity of visiting nearby Pitfour, only to be woken in the night with the news that the *Pylades* had broken her moorings and struck the Horseback Rocks. She was re-floated on the high tide the following day, but only after her masts had been cut away and her guns thrown overboard into the North Sea, where they probably still lie to this day. The badly damaged sloop was towed to a safe berth where she was repaired and, after several months, made seaworthy again. The Admiralty could not have been very pleased and although George was seemingly never reprimanded for the incident, it did his naval career little good. Although he was given a further command, the twenty-gunned HMS *Spey*, the cessation of the Napoleonic Wars marked the end of his naval career and in 1815, at the age of 27, he retired from the navy on half pay and with the rank of captain.

George married in 1812, but his first wife died in childbirth. In 1825 he remarried and between 1826 and 1835, he and new wife Elizabeth had five children, including a male heir, George Arthur (the 6th and last laird), in 1835. George, the 5th laird, had succeeded to the Pitfour Estates in 1821, by which time the seeds of his reckless style of living were well established. Buchan lore has it that the 5th laird came to Pitfour with debt and left Pitfour in debt. In 1822, he sold off several thousand acres of the Pitfour Estate, probably to pay off accumulated gambling debts from before his lairdship. Over the next few decades, he would gamble recklessly and spend thoughtlessly, before dying in 1867, thus permitting his son and heir to continue the process of draining the ancestral estate of worth and resources. George's changes included improving the access routes throughout Pitfour by driving roads from the main house to the various extremities of the estate. Lodge houses, complete with handsome wooden-colonnaded frontages, were built where the estate roads exited on to the public roads – at Fetterangus Road and the road to Strichen. Pitfour House then underwent extensive alterations. A new Home Farm was built at Cairnorchies and the old Home Farm demolished, to make way for a splendid stable block, complete with copper-domed clock tower and workers' accommodation.

A riding school followed and George then laid out the 16m-wide Pitfour racecourse. Locally known as the 'Ascot of the North', the route of the racecourse is nowadays largely hidden in forestry, but in its heyday the racetrack began some 400ft above sea level at Home Farm, before running for around 2 miles through White Cow Wood, Auchrynie and Cairnorchies. At points, the route traversed steep hillsides, requiring major civil engineering work in the form of cuttings and embankments, and when completed it must have been the wonder of the Buchan countryside.

THE LAIRD'S GOLDEN HORSESHOES

Perhaps the Admiral's most visible folly – restored by the former Banff and Buchan District Council and nowadays open to the public – was his erection of The Observatory at Drinnies Wood. Sited on the easterly slopes leading to the Home Farm, the white-painted, grey granite-and-brick tower sits almost 400ft above sea level and is some 50ft high. A popular myth tells that the tower was intended as a private viewing platform for the Admiral and his guests to view the races below, but this seems unlikely since the racetrack is some distance from the tower. It is more likely that the laird used the structure to gaze upon his property from above during his morning ride around the estate policies. The costs of building and manning an estate of such size and complexity were high. Fullarton's *Imperial Gazetteer of Scotland* for 1856 estimates that by that year, improvements to the grounds and mansion had cost the laird upwards of £80,000 and that the upkeep of the house and policies demanded an enormous staff. The *Gazetteer* comments that: 'Around the village of Deer is a plain of some considerable extent, ornamented with the woods and pleasure grounds of Pitfour.'

Foresters, factors, water bailiffs, gamekeepers and ploughmen worked the land, while butlers, footmen and cooks staffed the big house. There were stable men, kennel men and coachmen; lodge-keepers, gardeners and under-gardeners. In all, there must have been in excess of 100 estate employees, each of whom required payment, equipment and accommodation. No wonder the family's fortunes were in decline. Additionally, the Admiral's love of gambling and lavish entertaining only added to the outflow of wealth from the estate coffers. Local lore asserts that the laird's horses were shod with golden shoes.

In 1851, the Admiral's daughter, Eliza, a favourite, died aged just 21. In an act that at the time was seen as blatant vandalism, the Admiral decided to inter her at Deer Abbey. The destruction wrought to the Abbey during the building of a mausoleum to Eliza was later mirrored by his use of Pictish symbol stones from the building as infill during the upgrading of Saplinbrae House.

Deer Abbey (© Duncan Harley)

Some years after the laird's death, the mausoleum was torn down and a simple headstone now marks the grave of the unfortunate Eliza Ferguson. The Admiral died in 1867 and the 6th and final laird of Pitfour, George Arthur Ferguson, took over the running of the family estate.

A CRIMEAN COLONEL

The first three lairds could be fairly credited with the growing and improving of Pitfour. The 4th laird, George Ferguson, also added considerable value to the family coffers through his business interests, including ownership of sugar plantations in the Caribbean. The beginning of the decline in fortunes can be laid firmly at the door of the 5th and 6th lairds, who freely spent the family fortune and in doing so, eroded the estate's capital to the point of eventual bankruptcy. Now we turn to his son – yet another George – the 6th and last laird of Pitfour.

Known as the Colonel, George Arthur Ferguson had fought in the Crimea with the Grenadier Guards, aiding the Turks in their campaign against the Russians at both Alma and Sebastopol. He returned from war in 1856 and in February 1861 married Nina Maria Hood, a distant grand-niece of Horatio, Lord Nelson. The wedding took place in the Chapel at Windsor Castle, and there were great celebrations at Pitfour, with bonfires being lit across the whole of Buchan. At Pitfour, his father, George, laid on an elaborate dinner-dance for several hundred invited guests in the estate's riding school. Toasts of 'Here's health to young Pitfour' and 'Speed on the day that brings them here to see our Ugieside' rang out amid the firing of cannons in celebration of the marriage.

In all, there were eighteen toasts to the lucky couple *in absentia*, and it seems likely that the dancing portion of the event must have been spectacular indeed.

When his father died, in 1867, George Arthur Ferguson became the 6th and final laird of Pitfour. The Admiral had inherited an estate worth in excess of £300,000; four decades on, the Colonel was to inherit a much lesser sum, of perhaps £130,000, plus the responsibilities of the upkeep of a now decaying and neglected estate.

There was also the small matter of the £250,000 bond repayable to Scottish Widows Fund and Life, with interest accruing at 4 per cent per annum. A laird with some sound business sense and a good understanding of agricultural matters could probably have ridden the financial storm and eventually reversed the family fortunes for the better. However, the Colonel and his wife were more inclined to follow the extravagances of the 5th laird and, to this end, they hired a factor to carry out the day-to-day running of estate business, thus leaving themselves more time to enjoy the leisurely aspects of their elevated position.

Further loans were taken on and Pitfour House was subjected to a year-long renovation. The Colonel's wife, the

Hon. Nina Maria Hood, lost considerable sums of money at the gaming tables of fashionable casinos in both London and Monte Carlo.

More debts emerged, however. The family estates in Tobago, left by the 4th laird, were sequestrated by the island authorities due to an accumulation of unpaid taxes. The family mausoleum in Edinburgh's Greyfriars Churchyard required urgent repairs to prevent collapse and protect the incumbents from public gaze. The sorry list ran on and the decline of the family fortunes accelerated.

PITFOUR'S FINAL DECLINE

In the 1870s, a dispute broke out between Pitfour and the adjoining estate of Aden. Both estates were burdened by debt and, seemingly, there had been a history of animosity between the two for several years. The first trains from Mintlaw to Aberdeen ran in July 1861 and the line to Peterhead opened the following year, with the Fraserburgh line opening a few years later. The railway line through Maud cut through both estates and in some places parcels of land had become completely cut off from direct access by their respective owners.

In 1875, the laird of Aden Estate quite sensibly proposed that agreement be reached to simply exchange land in order to sort out these anomalies. He proposed to exchange Pitfour land south of the railway for Aden land over at Kininmonth. Inevitably, an argument broke out regarding the valuation of the parcels of land in question and, despite arbiters being appointed, neither side would agree to abide by the result of arbitration. A feud ensued and between 1875 and 1887, the two estates were to engage in a petty litigation game involving water rights, salmon fishing rights and even the course of the River Ugie.

The dispute was to end with the death of the Aden laird, James Russell. His successor reached an agreement with Pitfour in 1887. Common sense had prevailed and the war between the two neighbours was finally at an end.

However, Pitfour Estate fortunes continued to decline. Lady Ferguson – a Woman of the Bedchamber to Queen Victoria – continued to accrue huge gambling debts and at one point White Cow Wood was cut down in an effort to balance the books. On felling a particularly fine oak, an estate forester was heard to exclaim, 'There goes another for my lady.'

There was worse to come. Pitfour House, with its 365 windows, fifty-two rooms, four staircases and twelve portico pillars, was by now riddled with dry rot and required extensive remedial work. There was also a clamour among tenants for a general reduction in rents and, by 1879, the estate factor had to reduce these by 20 per cent. To make matters worse, local authorities in the north-east were insisting that the laird should make substantial improvements to estate workers' houses. The debts continued to mount. By 1905, the Colonel's fortune was estimated at a mere £7,750. In 1909, the end came with the drawing up of a trust deed intended to ring-fence what assets still remained, while the whole estate was put on the open market.

Pitfour Estate was bankrupt and the Fergusons had no choice but to sell to the highest bidder. There was little buying interest, however, and it took until 1926 to sell what remained of the Pitfour legacy. By the late 1920s, little remained apart from land and follies. The contents of Pitfour House were sold off piecemeal and the decaying building was demolished in 1928. Much of its stone was rumoured to have been used in the building of council housing in Aberdeen's Kincorth housing estate.

The Colonel, the 6th and last laird of Pitfour, spent his final years living between Pitfour and his property in

London. Saplinbrae House had been put at his disposal and Old Pittie, as the locals had nicknamed him, remained a familiar but perhaps sad figure in the Buchan countryside. Well known for his idiosyncrasies, he apparently had a particular dislike of cyclists and, given the opportunity, would poke his walking stick between the spokes of passing machines to fell the unfortunate rider. He remained remarkably active well into his later years and, during visits to the estate, he could sometimes be seen fishing in the Ugie. The Colonel died, insolvent, in Essex on 15 December 1924 and is buried alongside Nina Maria, at Luton.

Saplinbrae House (© Duncan Harley)

PITFOUR TODAY

Nowadays, the Pitfour Estate policies are popular with walkers, who no doubt gaze upon the surviving buildings and architectural follies with some wonder. Few perhaps realise that they are looking at the final remnants of a dynasty that, in the space of just over 200 years, had risen, flourished and foundered.

The grandly named Blenheim of Buchan is no more, and spectacular buildings such as the *circa* 1835 Temple of Theseus and the stunning 1820 neoclassical stable block are listed by Historic Scotland as being in critical condition.

A recent visit to Pitfour revealed that the copper-domed wooden clocktower above the stable block had collapsed into the forecourt, and that the Admiral's alligator pond within the temple had all but disappeared under the weight of debris from the disintegrating roof. In 2012, Aberdeenshire Council gave the go-ahead for restoration work on the temple. Funding was expected to come via planning gain from the construction of several luxury houses on the Pitfour Estate. In consequence bridges around the estate policies have been repaired and re-pointed and a network of paths has been formed around Pitfour Lake. At the time of writing, however, the historic Temple of Theseus still awaits the kind hand of the restorer and George Ferguson's alligators may soon have to look for a new home.

5

TURNPIKE MANIA

Turnpikes have been described as one of the central pillars on which the Industrial and Agricultural Revolution was based and there is some truth in this assertion. In Aberdeenshire, as in the rest of Scotland, various Parliamentary Turnpike Acts spawned a new improved road system that was to lead to better communications, more efficient movement of goods and easier importation of raw materials and agricultural inputs. The eighteenth century saw the old system where responsibility for the county's roads moved from local Commissioners of Supply to a system based on road-funding via tolls levied on road users. The old system relied on tenants turning out on specified days to labour for free on the county's roads. Those choosing to forgo this obligation could pay a fine or indeed employ a neighbour as a stand-in.

This system of statute labour had its problems. Various reports in the Statistical Accounts point to a poor standard of roadmaking. The minister at Drumblade, for example, complained that a sparse population who showed a disinclination to work on the highways combined with a shortage of suitable road-making materials had led to 'a quite inadequate situation which was moreover supervised by partial or negligent overseers'. Additionally, steep gradients that were only useable to wheeled carriages during 'a sparse few months in summer' led to a situation where the old method of drawing goods by horse and sled remained the only practical method of moving large loads during most of the year. The advent of the tollbooth funded turnpike system was to change all of that.

The county's first turnpike was driven along the north bank of the River Dee and linked Aberdeen with Drum, a distance of some 12 miles. Tollgates were set up and investors included Irvine of Drum and the Earl of Aboyne. Work began at Mannofield in 1796 and the road was completed two years later. Eventually, the turnpikes extended right across the county, linking key settlements such as Ellon, Fraserburgh, Turriff and Inverurie to Aberdeen. There were many problems, not the least of them financial. Long-winded legal disputes also held up the progress of the new roads. One landowner, Alexander Shand of Tanfield, was reported to have been particularly awkward.

He seemingly accosted the road gang who were quite legitimately engaged in laying the turnpike across his land. After confiscating their tools, he ordered them off the land and made complaints to the road trustees, claiming that they had been abusing their authority by misapplying funds. After a long and embittered legal battle, the controversy was resolved in favour of the turnpike commissioners and the improved road over Shand's land went ahead as planned.

As it turned out, the turnpikes were to be a short-term solution to the county's transport needs and the tollgates were soon redundant, although virtually every town and village in Aberdeenshire could at one time boast a tollhouse amongst its housing stock. By 1805 or thereabouts, most routes out from Aberdeen had been improved and it was possible to travel around the shire at speed. Inverness could be reached from Aberdeen in around 18 hours and Edinburgh to Aberdeen took perhaps a day and a half. However, the days of Turnpike Mania were to be short-lived and soon Canal Mania and Railway Mania were to take on the mantle of economic improvement. Even today, the turnpike tollhouses, some 120 of them, guard the roadways along the major roads throughout the north-east. In vogue for some three decades at the very most, the quaintly constructed toll-keeper's dwellings, with their distinctive bay front designed to give the toll-collector a clear view of the road, serve to remind us of the early and short-lived attempts to improve trade and communications in the pre-Victorian era.

6

CANAL MANIA

Widespread flooding caused by Storm Frank in late 2015 launched Port Elphinstone, Inverurie's 'Port in the Country', into the national headlines for all the wrong reasons. When the River Don burst its banks and overflowed into the streets and houses of the Inverurie suburb, news crews from major networks including the BBC and Sky broadcast a story of wrecked homes and disrupted lives. However, despite clues in the form of street names such as Canal Crescent and Canal View, few news reports acknowledged the inland port's links with that 200-year-old waterway, the Aberdeenshire Canal. Opened in 1805, the trade route operated until mid-1854 when new owners, the Great North of Scotland Railway, began work on the railway line linking Aberdeen to Inverness.

The concept of moving heavy goods by canal became popular in Scotland around 1800. The Forth and Clyde Canal had opened in 1790, the Crinan Canal in 1801 and the Caledonian Canal in 1822. Archibald Grant of Monymusk, among others, had floated the idea of an Aberdeenshire Canal in about 1790 and in 1793 a survey was commissioned to map a route for a proposed Don and Urie-side Canal. The original idea had been to follow the courses of the rivers Don and Urie to link Insch and Monymusk with Inverurie and Aberdeen Harbour. There was even a suggestion that the water-network might include the settlements of Aboyne and Banchory. However, following the survey, a less ambitious route linking Inverurie to Aberdeen roughly along the line of the River Don was adopted.

The rise of the railway as a means of transportation was some years away and despite the advent of the turnpikes, moving bulky or heavy goods such as granite, grain and fertilisers to and from the seaport at Aberdeen remained expensive and difficult. Despite the obvious benefits of water-borne transportation, funding proved problematic and when digging began in 1798, only £17,715 of the eventual £43,895 construction cost had been raised. On top of the funding deficit, disputes with landowners along the proposed route proved costly both in time and money. At one point, in a scenario familiar to the planners of the modern-day Aberdeen ring road, the Sheriff Depute of Aberdeenshire had to intervene to settle a long-running dispute over compensation due to a Pitmedden landowner for the requisition of his land.

The Aberdeenshire Canal at Port Elphinstone (© Duncan Harley)

Eventually, following the sale of further share options and the mortgaging of the lease of the tolls, work was completed and on Wednesday, 5 June 1805 the new waterway officially opened for business. Following an opening ceremony at the canal basin at Inverurie, the *Aberdeen Journal* describes the official first trip to Aberdeen in glowing terms. Dignitaries including the Lord Provost of Aberdeen and local magistrates boarded the horse-drawn passenger barge *The Countess of Kintore*, which was 'handsomely decorated and fitted up' for the voyage of 'seven hours and a half'. As the barge made its way down to Aberdeen, crowds of curious spectators lined the banks while 'a gun fixed to the prow of the vessel was fired occasionally' to announce its approach. The article reveals that the canal had actually been in operation for a short period prior to the opening ceremony. At least one barge had already delivered a cargo of coal to Port Elphinstone and another had transported fertiliser to Kintore. Business was already looking good.

TEETHING PROBLEMS AND HARBOUR ACCESS

There were teething problems. Kintore was a major port on the canal route and the waterway ran directly through the town's streets. Shortly prior to the official commissioning of the canal, an embankment on the outskirts of town collapsed and a wall of water engulfed the settlement. Some residents at the lower end of town sought safety by climbing through the thatched roofs of their cottages. At the Aberdeen end, several canal locks suffered structural failure not long after the commissioning. Described as poorly built, these had to be re-engineered, necessitating the temporary closure of the canal. By October 1806 the repairs, supervised by Thomas Telford, were complete and the canal was reopened.

Cold winter weather was an ongoing issue and movement was restricted between December and May. The canal was shallow with an average depth of about 3.5ft and often froze over. Additionally, towpaths tended to ice over in winter, making the task of the motive power – horses – dangerous and difficult. There were also ongoing issues affecting the cost-effectiveness and convenience of the venture. During the initial twenty-nine years of operation there was no direct sea access for canal barges at Aberdeen Harbour. Cargo required to be offloaded then stored prior to trans-shipment onto seagoing vessels. This additional expense and delay eventually resulted in a sea lock being built in 1834, at a cost of £1,500, enabling canal barges to berth alongside seagoing vessels. The barges could only enter or leave the harbour according to the tides, but the benefits were obvious. As the *Aberdeen Journal* pointed out, 'Country distillers, by making Port Elphinstone their place of shipment will effect a very great saving in their charges for carriage. Stone merchants will save the whole expense of stone stances.' The most time-consuming portion of the journey was the stretch between Stoneywood and the harbour at Aberdeen. The canal followed a contour along the general course of the River Don as far as the outskirts of the city, where the cutting veered away from the river. There were seventeen locks between Port Elphinstone and the harbour at Aberdeen, with the water level at Inverurie estimated by some sources as being 170ft above the level of the basin at Aberdeen. Crucially, all of the locks lay between Stoneywood and the harbour – a distance of almost 5 miles – forcing traffic to navigate a drop of around 168ft in seventeen time-consuming stages. A typical waterborne journey from Inverurie's Port Elphinstone to the outskirts of the Aberdeen took just over three hours, with passenger journeys generally ending at the Kittybrewster Boathouse, having passed through the first three canal locks at Stoneywood, Waterton Road and Great Northern Road.

The journey through the remaining fourteen locks down to Waterloo Quay took a further three hours, which goods traffic had to endure. Passengers heading into the city could cover the distance between the Boathouse and the harbour terminus in less than twenty minutes by coach.

THE SIGNIFICANCE OF THE ABERDEENSHIRE CANAL

At just over 18 miles in length, the Aberdeenshire Canal appears insignificant when compared to the Union Canal's 31 miles and the 35-mile-long Forth and Clyde Canal but, in terms of impact on the agricultural and industrial economy of Aberdeenshire and the City of Aberdeen, the undertaking proved to be equally as important as those loftier and better-known waterways. Port Elphinstone owes its very existence to the canal. In pre-canal days there would have been one or two crofts on the land. When the canal came, the landscape sprouted wharves and warehouses plus associated housing for workers. There was at least one grain mill and there are remnants of what may have been a bone-mill.

Further down the route towards Aberdeen, settlements such as Kintore became important staging posts both for the import and export of goods and as livery points for the horses that hauled the barges to and from Aberdeen. The Annals of Aberdeen record that in 1808 there were seventeen barges plus two flyboats – or passenger boats – employed on the canal, which indicates the scale of the enterprise. Exports included heavy goods such as granite and slate alongside wheat and oats. In 1833 alone over 2,180 tons of stone and 461 tons of slate – presumably extracted from the slate quarries at Colpy – left Port Elphinstone on the journey south to Aberdeen. In the same year 2,829 tons of lime, 2,184 tons of coal and 102 tons of dung – possibly the night soil of the City of Aberdeen – made the journey north to Inverurie. Imports of bones for fertilizer amounted to 278 tons in 1835. By 1838 this figure had reached 1,394 tons, hence the need for the bone-mill at Port Elphinstone. Clearly the lime, dung and bone meal were key inputs to the agricultural prosperity of Aberdeenshire.

Interestingly, the figure for the import of dung, known in polite circles as night soil, peaked in 1837 at a massive 1,642 tons before decreasing the following year to a mere 670 tons. Night soil is a euphemism for human and animal faeces collected nightly from cesspools and privies. Utilised as fertilizer, it was prized by farmers and there are contemporary accounts of a ton of the noxious stuff costing 12 shillings following transportation from Aberdeen to Inverurie. One account mentions the importation into Aberdeenshire of night soil all the way from London via Aberdeen docks that might, on further investigation, explain the 1837 spike in imports.

THE ABERDEENSHIRE CANAL TODAY

The canal nowadays is most evident at Port Elphinstone, where a complete section survives relatively intact. Other sections, such as that on Aberdeen's Great Northern Road at the Haudagain roundabout, today resemble little more than a wide dry ditch. Much of the remainder of the canal bed, especially in Aberdeen city, has disappeared completely under both the railway line linking Inverurie to Aberdeen and the various housing developments that have taken place over the past two centuries. Some sources assert that the construction of the Great North of Scotland Railway obliterated the canal route and while in places this was the case, probably slightly less than 6 miles of the entire 17-mile length of the canal bed was actually utilised by the Victorian railway engineers. Even today, stretches of drained canal bed are clearly visible both around Kintore and alongside the Great Northern Road in Aberdeen.

In addition to the seventeen canal locks, there were several aqueducts and an estimated fifty bridges crossed the canal at various points along the route. Modern-day travellers heading into Aberdeen on the A96 are probably unaware of the archaeology lying alongside the carriageway at locations such as Warrack's Bridge on Station Road, Woodside, where the course of the original waterway is clearly visible both underneath and on both sides of the bridge.

Relics including half-mile markers lie at various points along the route. Used as way-points and as a means of levying carriage charges, they can be seen at Stoneywood's Polo Park, Dyce Caravans yard and, until quite recently, in the front garden of Bridgend House at Kintore. Nearer Aberdeen city centre the canal survives mainly in the form of street names such as Canal Street, Canal Road and Canal Terrace. There are probably no remaining traces above ground at Waterloo Quay.

ABERDEENSHIRE'S CANAL ART

Two artworks – 'The Port Arch' (2004) by Gordon Lochhead and the Millennium-funded granite-built 'Memorial to the Aberdeenshire Canal' by Inverurie stonemasons including Karl Bisset – mark the Inverurie end of the canal and archaeological remains at Port Elphinstone include a half-mile stretch of waterway, a canal bridge, plus remnants of the harbour basin. Additionally, the skeleton of what may well be an original iron canal inspection boat from around 1805 lies rusting amongst bushes alongside the River Don at Port Elphinstone, having been retrieved from the canal bank by a local mill-worker.

The memorial sculpture at Port Elphinstone incorporates a stone lintel said by some to have come from the lintel quarry on the slopes of the nearby Bennachie hill range. Abandoned in the nineteenth century after the quarry access track was washed away in a flood, the lintel quarry still contains a number of finely cut granite lintel stones alongside the quarry face. It had been the intention of the stonemasons to use one of these lintels as a part of the artwork; however, plans had to be altered when objections were raised by the Forestry Commission. So, instead of using historic granite from Millstone Hill, a recycled lintel was sourced elsewhere. Said stone was duly hauled by sled and brute force all the way up the hill to the old quarry, then hauled all the way back down again to be incorporated into the sculpture, thus allowing the team of masons to claim that the lintel had come from the Bennachie lintel quarry.

'The Port Arch' sculpture by Gordon Lochhead (© Duncan Harley)

Many canals have in recent years been revived and utilised for leisure purposes. The Falkirk Wheel at the junction of the Forth and Clyde and Union Canals is a major tourist draw and the 30m-high Kelpies sculpture on the Forth and Clyde Canal extension attracted a million visitors in its first year alone. Proving perhaps that possibilities are limited only by imagination, Turner Prize-nominated artist Roger Hiorns seems poised to revive the fortunes of the Birmingham canal system by burying an entire passenger jet – you can pick one up as scrap for a mere £50,000 – alongside a twenty-first-century canal-side housing and retail development.

The Aberdeenshire Canal is nowadays a largely neglected local asset. Perhaps the time is right to develop the route for leisure purposes. The burying of aeroplanes might be a step too far but perhaps a Kelpie or two might be in order.

Nowadays of course, navigation along Scotland's remaining 140-mile-long canal network is only possible due to government inputs. The Scottish Government contributes some £11m per year in subsidies for what is nowadays viewed primarily as a tourist asset. Despite some 85,000 boat movements per year on the likes of the Crinan and Caledonian Canals, the heady days of canal mania are gone forever.

7

RAILWAY MANIA

The Aberdeenshire Canal gave way to the railways and indeed in many places the Victorian railway into Aberdeen from Inverurie closely follows the route laid out by the canal engineers. Steam engines such as Stephenson's Rocket had, of course, pioneered the railway trend and it was not long before the iconic Rocket, with its curmudgeonly top speed of 12mph, was superseded by more ambitious designs. Sixty miles an hour was soon achieved and some folk, including Queen Victoria, feared that the very act of breathing in air at such speeds might prove fatal. The railway brought new prosperity to the shire and enabled fast access to markets across Britain and far beyond. Fisher towns such as Fraserburgh and Peterhead benefited greatly from the coming of the railway.

In *The A–Z of Curious Aberdeenshire* I wrote about the arrival of Buffalo Bill's Wild West Show in Fraserburgh in August 1904. The showmen set up on the Links having unloaded their 500 horses and 800 or so performers from three specially chartered trains, which had arrived in the early hours from Peterhead. Part of a nationwide and European tour, the one-day halt to perform at the Broch would not have been possible were it not for the railway network. The same railway that brought Buffalo Bill to the Broch had, of course, been instrumental in the increasingly rapid growth of Fraserburgh in the years following the northern extension of the Great North of Scotland Railway to the town in 1865. When the first steam train was run on the line in the April of that year, thousands of folks who had perhaps never seen a train before descended on the Broch to see the opening ceremony and indulge in cheap introductory fares offered by the railway company. The railways soon caught on and although they must have had a detrimental effect on the coastal steamer trade to and from the local harbours, the speed and efficiency of rail transport brought many benefits to the towns along the line.

Railway Mania (© Duncan Harley)

In the boom fishing years of the nineteenth and early twentieth centuries the railways not only transported produce out of Fraserburgh to the UK but also brought in the workforce needed to process the annual herring harvest. David Toulmin in his short story 'The Last Journey' provides a first-class account of the boom and bust of the Buchan rail lines. He writes eloquently that, 'At the height of the herring season upwards of twenty-one fish trains left Fraserburgh daily ... but by 1928 the engines on the Buchan line were having an easier time.'

By the 1960s demand had fallen off again despite a short recovery during the Second World War and in 1965 passenger services were finally withdrawn, with freight traffic continuing until 1979. Nowadays the Buchan railway line is better known to cyclists and walkers as the 53-mile-long Formartine and Buchan Way, linking Dyce to Peterhead and Fraserburgh. The population of Fraserburgh in pre-railway 1840 was recorded as 3,080 and by 1901 this had increased to 9,715. In around 1880, following significant harbour investment including the construction of a new breakwater, Fraserburgh had emerged as the Scottish Herring Capital, overtaking the popularity of both Wick and Peterhead. Period photographs show the harbour filled with literally hundreds of fishing boats. It might not be a leap of faith to credit the rail network for that newfound prosperity.

THE RAILWAY TO ELLON

Similarly, the inland town of Ellon owes much of its prosperity to the arrival of the steam age. The armies of Robert the Bruce had changed the face of Ellon completely during what came to be known as the 'Harrying of Buchan', or the 'Herschip of Buchaine'. By all accounts the Bruce was a nasty piece of work. Accompanied by his brother Edward he laid waste to the whole of Buchan. Alongside the burning of crofts and crops, he put entire families to the sword and ensured that the few surviving inhabitants lost all loyalty to his foes. Buchan folk bemoaned the devastation and some took to verse. Churchman John Barbour recorded the violent act of destruction:

And gert his men bryn all Buchaine,
Fra end till end and sparyt nane,
And heryit thaim in sic maneir,
That eftre that weile fifty year,
Men meynt the herschip of Buchaine.

In more enlightened times, improvements in agriculture and communication revived Ellon's fortunes and when the railway arrived, in 1861, the Buchan capital's position as a prosperous market town was firmly cemented. Nowadays, only the Station Hotel survives to remind us of the days when the railway station bustled with both passenger and freight traffic, and it is difficult to fully appreciate the effect rail transportation had on the local economy.

Mail, livestock, coal, crops and even newspapers moved swiftly over the rail network. New markets opened up and Ellon prospered. As always, technology moved on and by the 1920s roads had improved to the point where the motor truck and local buses could compete with the railways. By then, the old road bridge over the River Ythan was deemed in urgent need of replacement. With a roadway a mere 16ft wide, it seemed quite unsuited to the needs of modern motor transport. Retained as a pedestrian bridge, running alongside the modern road bridge, it had been completed in 1793, after two years of construction, and remains today the last-surviving example of the work of Banff mason James Robertson, being similar in design to his 1791 bridge over the Don in Inverurie, which was demolished in 1924.

Records held by the Royal Commission on the Ancient and Historical Monuments of Scotland indicate that following Robertson's completion of the Inverurie bridge over the Don, the timber shuttering used to form the arches was floated down the River Don, shipped north to Newburgh, then floated up the River Ythan for re-use in the construction of Ellon's Auld Brig.

River traffic had been navigating the Ythan between the port of Newburgh and the Meadows, 4 miles upstream, since at least the fifteenth century and the river remained navigable to medium-sized coastal boats until fairly recent times. During the nineteenth and twentieth centuries, barges laden with agricultural lime and coal were towed upstream from Newburgh to the Meadows just south of Ellon by shallow-draft, steam-driven paddle tugs, such as the wonderfully named SS *Despatch*. Nowadays river traffic has ceased completely and both the port at Newburgh and the railhead in Ellon town centre are but distant memories.

THE RAILWAY AT ABOYNE

For almost half a century, the Deeside village of Aboyne marked the end of the turnpike road from Aberdeen. By the 1850s, however, pressure from local stagecoach operators and commercial carriers led to the extension of the turnpike as far west as Braemar. Earlier landowners and local visionaries had considered the digging of a grand canal linking Aboyne with Aberdeen but this project failed to gain popular support due to engineering issues, including the need for costly aqueducts. Alongside road improvements there was a need for improved river crossings. There were many ferries operating on the Dee, most were small craft operated by local entrepreneurs – sometimes called 'Boaties' – who for a small fee would row folk across the river. The ferry at Aboyne was typical of the breed and crossed the Dee near the Old Boat Inn on Charleston Road.

The boatie ferry at Aboyne operated until 1827 when a tragic accident, during the October St Michael Fair, occurred.

Despite a sudden spate, the boatman left the north bank with his heavily overloaded boat crammed to the gunwales with late-night revellers. Near the south side, the ferry overturned and all on board were thrown into the water. Most scrambled ashore but a woman and her daughter drowned. Word of the tragedy reached Aboyne some three hours later, when the boatman himself brought the news having hiked 12 miles back to Aboyne via the Potarch Bridge.

The incident prompted the then Earl of Aboyne to fund a suspension bridge over the river. The present Aboyne bridge is the fourth to be built on the site. For a brief period after the railway arrived in 1859, the town became the railhead of the Royal Deeside Line. Aboyne found itself playing host to Queen Victoria, her entourage and her distinguished visitors as they disembarked from royal trains to stop over at the likes of the Huntly Arms – perhaps Scotland's oldest coaching inn – before travelling on to Balmoral Castle by road. With the arrival of the Deeside Railway to the town, agricultural goods, foodstuffs and of course timber, which in pre-railway days had been floated down the Dee, now gravitated to the railways. Steam trains slashed journey times and as transport costs decreased tourism began to increase.

The combination of Sir Walter Scott's romanticised tales of broadsword-wielding tartan-clad Highlanders plus the attraction of hunting, shooting and fishing proved irresistible and attracted hordes of tourists intent on sampling the Highland lifestyle. Aboyne benefited greatly and Queen Victoria's royal romance with the Highlands added value to the Deeside brand. By the time of her death in 1901 the town's population had more than doubled from a pre-railway 1841 figure of just 260 to 561. The 2011 Census records 2,602 residents. George Bradshaw's General Railway and Steam Navigation Guide for 1863 records that Aboyne station 'offers an excellent starting point for the tourist to visit the picturesque scenery extending between Ballater, Braemar and Balmoral'. Clearly George was intent on disturbing the monarch's peace and quiet. Alongside the more traditional sporting pursuits, today's visitors to Aboyne can engage in outdoor activities undreamed of by their nineteenth- and twentieth-century forebears. Off-road 4x4 experiences, Deeside Way walking tours and wildlife safaris vie with artistic and cultural activity for the tourist pound. Aboyne Highland Games (now into its 148th year), the Aboyne and Deeside Festival and Active Aboyne 2015 complement the experience of visiting what is in effect a Victorian country resort elevated to twenty-first-century status. Situated on the very edge of the Cairngorm National Park – the largest in the UK – and with the magnificent 25,000-acre Glen Tanar estate literally on the doorstep, the town is steeped in centuries of rich history and offers both visitors and locals alike a unique Royal Deeside experience.

When the Deeside railway line finally closed in 1966 the old station buildings were retained and converted into shops and business units. Even the old rail tunnel running from the station under the town centre found new use as an underground rifle range.

Although the Deeside Railway has gone, possibly for good, a nostalgic nod towards the steam age has been retained at Aboyne's Boat Inn, where a scale model steam engine runs regular scheduled services between the lounge and the public bar. The experience is quite surreal, especially after a pie and a pint.

THE RAILWAY THROUGH INSCH

The Garioch town of Insch somehow managed to retain its railway station despite the reshaping of the railway system following the Beeching Reports of the 1960s and today provides rural commuters with fast access to the Oil Capital of Europe, and, in addition, hosts a community-run museum in the former ticket office.

Insch Connection Museum, a Registered Scottish Charity, hold an extensive archive relating to Insch's past. The museum's focus for 2016 was 'Souters of Insch', a family business once central to Insch's economy. Trading in everything from fencing supplies to wedding presents, the Souter brand was instrumental in bringing both electricity and employment to the village and for over ninety years operated a popular general goods store on Commercial Road. The town today boasts an aerodrome, a manufacturer of landmine clearance machines, plus a good selection of archaeology. It can also claim the distinction of being one of only a few places in Scotland bombed by the Germans in the First World War.

Perhaps oddly, Bradshaw's Railway Guide makes scant reference to the Garioch village, commenting only that 'Insch, close to which is Craigievar, is the seat of Sir W. Forbes, Bart; here fairs are held on Friday.' Writing in around 1863, Bradshaw obviously was completely unaware that the very first section of the Great North of Scotland Railway linking Aberdeen to Inverness was laid just 2 miles down the line at Westhall Estate following the cutting of the first sod by Lady Elphinstone in November 1852.

THE RAILWAY AT TORPHINS

The picturesque settlement of Torphins lies roughly 22 miles west of Aberdeen, around 18 miles from Ballater and just a couple of miles from the site of Macbeth's last stand at Lumphanan in August 1057. While neighbouring settlements such as Kincardine O'Neil, Tarland and Tornaveen struggled economically during the 1800s, the completion of the Royal Deeside Railway's Aboyne Extension in 1859 gave Torphins a golden key to economic growth. The Deeside Railway initially opened as a single-track line linking Aberdeen to Banchory in September 1853. The Upper Deeside Extension to Aboyne followed in

December 1859 and a further extension to Ballater became operational in 1866. Although the original plan involved running the line through Kincardine O'Neil, the eventual route diverted to the north and away from the River Dee, running through both Torphins and Lumphanan and involved the laying of an extra 2 miles of track.

A claim at the time was that the deviation from plan had saved money by economising on land purchase and construction costs but this seems dubious since the gradients, in an era when long inclines were a serious problem for steam trains, on both sides of the Torphins loop involved major groundwork. A more likely explanation, familiar to the residents of the Moray Coast town of Cullen where the Countess of Seafield's refusal to allow the trains to cross her estate left the townsfolk cowering beneath a series of vast railway viaducts, is that one Deeside landowner simply refused to release the land required by the railway engineers while another, more enlightened laird, welcomed the permanent way with open palms.

The railway route through Torphins avoided major disruption to the existing settlement and there were few issues such as those at neighbouring Lumphanan, where Kirktown of Lumphanan was not only left stranded a good half mile from the railway station but was, according to Deeside historian G.M. Fraser, 'cut off from the church itself by the intervening railway line'. The railway certainly delivered prosperity to Torphins and even today a brief wander around the village reveals a number of solidly constructed granite ex-railway buildings nowadays converted for use as dwellings.

A reminder of the village's railway history is Platform 22 on Station Road. Multitasking as a licensed bistro, a gallery space for local artists and a popular cosy café, Platform 22 is situated on the site of the original railway station and although, according to joint owner and ceramicist Emma Pattullo, little apart from a few scattered stones from the original platform remain, the café with its nostalgic railway signage is clearly a hub of village life.

Used as a military recruiting centre during the First World War and sited on a plot gifted by the Learney Estate, the village's 1899 granite-built Learney Hall plays host to a wide range of community events including fundraisers for the local amateur football club, fashion shows, Breakneck Comedy Club and events connected to the annual Torphins Gala. A recent highlight was a talk by 1988 Calgary Winter Olympics ski-jump superstar Eddie the Eagle.

Opposite the hall sits the distinctive Star and Griffin. Bearing the coat of arms of the Learney family, the building was once a popular stopping-off place for both rail travellers and Deeside tourists. Known far and wide as the 'Sunshine Café', the structure nowadays doubles as a family home and pre-school nursery.

Just over the road from the Star and Griffin is the Learney Arms Hotel. Functioning as a station hotel, the Learney Arms welcomed several unexpected guests during the winter of 1929. Three German hot-air balloonists had been blown off course during the short trip from Leipzig to Hanover, a distance of some 134 miles. An epic 1,000-mile nineteen-hour voyage over France and then across the North Sea ensued. Finally, the exhausted men crash-landed at Claydykes Farm near Tornaveen and were duly transported by road to Torphins for rest and recuperation prior to repatriation by rail to Leipzig.

ALFORD RAILHEAD

In July 1896 the folk of Alford witnessed the arrival, by train, of what was perhaps the first motor car to be driven down Alford's Main Street. A new Daimler Motor Horseless Carriage had arrived in town. The Locomotive Act of 1865 had recently been amended to permit motoring speeds of up to 12mph and drivers were no longer limited to 4mph on rural roads or 2mph in built-up areas. This led to a dramatic increase in car ownership in Aberdeenshire amongst those who saw the benefits of switching from horse-drawn to petrol-driven transport. The four-seater Daimler had been purchased by a Strathdon doctor and was delivered to Alford by Daimler chief engineer Otto Meyer. The *Aberdeen Journal* commented on the vehicle's 'easy running and the control the driver had over it'.

The town's Alford Valley Railway Line was built originally to facilitate the export of granite from local quarries such as that at Kemnay and Tillyfourie, and also the importation of manure via Aberdeen docks. The 16-mile-long spur line opened in 1859 without much fuss or celebration and the line, which linked Alford to the mainline at Kintore, operated for just over 100 years. Passenger traffic ended in 1950 and the line finally closed in 1966. As was the case with many settlements in the north-east, the railway was instrumental in both growing the existing settlement and relocating the town centre near the rail head.

There are local tales, possibly apocryphal, of travellers in pre-railway times asking the way to Alford only to be told that they were in the place already! When the railway came everything changed. By the late nineteenth century Aberdeenshire was producing over 300,000 tons of granite per year and towns such as Alford, which had not benefited much from the cutting of the Inverurie to Aberdeen canal, found a new prosperity with quarried Tillyfourie stone being exported by rail for use in the likes of London's Thames Embankment, Tower Bridge and HM Theatre Aberdeen.

Nowadays, a heritage Alford Valley Railway operates as a narrow-gauge line running through Haughton Country Park. The line, maintained and operated by volunteers, was opened in 1980, employing salvaged track and equipment from the redundant New Pitsligo peat moss railway.

Local lore insists that the original Victorian era Alford Valley line between Kintore Junction and the Alford terminus involved the steam engines making long and often painfully slow journeys up the steep incline between

Whitehouse and Tillyfourie. One often repeated tale recalls that some local wag had scrawled 'Please do not pick the daisies while the train is in motion!' on one of the carriage doors. Worse still, a further tale recalls a railway guard's infamous full-volume shout to those travelling on to Alford from Kintore, which sounded something like 'Kintore Junction! Change here for AAfert!'

PORTSOY'S HARBOUR LINE

Ironically, the railway was instrumental in killing off the harbour traffic in Portsoy. Nowadays a bustling coastal resort town and popular stopover on the 6,200km-long North Sea Cycle Route, Portsoy at one time boasted a herring fleet of some fifty-seven boats. Home for a time to author Peter Anson, co-founder of the Apostleship of the Sea and 'a skeely drawer o' boats an' haibers an' fisher fowk' according to one local fisherman, Portsoy in 1936 gained international fame as the home port of the drifter *Boy Andrew*, which that year won the Prunier Trophy with a catch of 231 crans. The prize, instituted by Parisian restaurant owner Madame Simone Prunier, was awarded annually to the drifter netting the highest crannage of herring in one shot and, alongside the trophy, involved the crew being invited to dine at her fashionable London restaurant, all expenses paid.

Uncharacteristically, Anson writes acidly of the win: 'It seems strange that it should need the enterprising proprietress of a fashionable London restaurant to bring Portsoy onto the national headlines.' As steam drifters gradually took over from the more traditional sail-driven Zulus and Skaffies during the late nineteenth century, harbour traffic declined and the majority of local boats gravitated to the larger harbours such as Buckie, Fraserburgh and Macduff. By the end of the nineteenth century the town's role as a seaport had also declined, killed off in part at least by the railways. A branch line from Tillynaught connected the harbour to the Great North of Scotland Railway main line at Grange but the completion of the Moray Coast Line in May 1886 effectively made the Portsoy Harbour extension with its steep 1:30 gradient redundant. Coastal trade in general merchandise, grain and timber moved to the larger north-east ports, where movement of goods by rail was much easier, and by 1910 the Portsoy harbour line had closed. A final death blow was dealt to Portsoy's harbour trade when the outbreak of the First World War severed the town's links with former European trading partners.

When columnist Cuthbert Graham wrote about Portsoy in 1963 he commented that the town was one of the most progressive communities on the Moray Firth. In his weekend travel column 'This is My Country', he wrote about the 'triumphant success' of the town's efforts to encourage tourism and the discussions then taking place regarding the rehabilitation of Loch Soy.

In the days before the advent of ice-making on a commercial basis, ice for the preserving of Scottish fish was either shipped in from places such as Greenland via the international ice trade or more likely harvested locally from ponds and rivers during the winter months. Portsoy's Loch Soy was at one time the main source of ice for the local salmon fishing industry and also provided water power for local mills such as MacDonald Brothers.

By the mid-twentieth century, however, the loch had become a weed-strewn eyesore and the local Town Improvement Association stepped in to address the issue. Following extensive landscaping, Loch Soy was officially reopened as a leisure park and boating loch in June 1973. The MacDonald Brothers mill had closed in 1968. In operation for around 112 years, the company operated as an engineering business complete with foundry and at its peak employed over twenty engineers, craftsmen and draughtsmen. Catering largely for the needs of fisher folk, MacDonald's patented a number of innovative designs, including one for a 'patented twin screw auxiliary propeller' driven by the same coal-fuelled engine employed for the boat's steam capstan.

This innovative design was intended to solve the problem of boats becoming becalmed. The *Banffshire Reporter* in May 1902 recorded how 'this invention … makes it possible for a boat to move at a speed of 3 to 4 knots an hour when a favourable breeze fails to fill the sails … we venture to state that many a fisherman, when wind fails him, may be enabled to realise from a night's shot considerably more than the little expense his propelling gear has cost him.'

Perhaps the factory's best-known innovation is the MacDonald Steam Capstan. As the need for herring drifters to venture further offshore led to the building of larger boats, so the difficulties of both hauling in nets and raising ever larger sails increased. The larger drifters had masts over 60ft in height and the effort of manually hauling the heavy sails up, especially in a breeze, was an exhausting job for all hands. The patented MacDonald Steam Capstan took the heavy work in its stride and very soon became an international success. Although competing companies manufactured similar products, the innovative reverse gear and ease of operation of the MacDonald model made it the market leader.

The Scottish Fisheries Museum's Fifie sailing herring drifter *Reaper* (FR 958) sports perhaps the very last of the 'Made in Portsoy' MacDonald Steam Capstans. Now converted to operate using compressed air, this example is in regular use on the Sandhaven-built boat, which is now part of the Core Collection of the National Historic Ships Fleet.

However, despite the MacDonald designs being employed all around the east coast and beyond, the harbour railway line at Portsoy vanished forever many years ago, leaving few traces apart from a trackless railway bed leading week-end tourists from the historic High Street down the brae to the old harbour. The fishing, the harbour trade and the railways have all in their turn come and gone forever.

8

THE PAINTING PRIEST OF MACDUFF

The late George Murdoch, a resident of the 'Local Hero' village of Pennan on the north-east coast, wrote shortly before he died on the history of a remarkable man, the artist, writer and churchman Peter Anson. 'The tea-room,' writes George, 'is faur Peter Anson had his hoose'. The harbourside café, of course, occupied the site of Anson's Loft Chapel at No. 2 Low Shore at Macduff.

Readers of my previous book, *The A–Z of Curious Aberdeenshire*, will recall that Peter's 'little cathedral of the north' was torn down by the forces of progress during the course of essential harbour extensions a few years after his death in 1975:

> Within this cramped fisherman's cottage, Peter had created a small chapel in the attic which at the time was the only Catholic place of worship in the entire town. Peter's home had already become an open house for visiting seamen and was a gathering place for many youngsters in the town. Affectionately known as 'Harbour Head' in his writings, it was to be Peter's home for fifteen years. The oratory, dedicated to Our Lady of the Ships and St Peter the Fisherman, was for many years also the only chapel on the Scottish mainland dedicated to the spiritual needs of mariners. Harbour Head's Loft Chapel sported an altar made by local joiner Geordie Watt and a canvas altar cover sewn from rough sail-cloth by Jim

Blair, the local sail-maker. On leaving Macduff, in 1952, Anson dismantled the oratory and shipped the contents to France for re-use by the Mission de la Mer.

Macduff, of course, is much the poorer for the act of municipal vandalism that led to the tearing down of Anson's residence. Imagine if you will the hordes of visitors who might, if things had been different, have descended on the town intent on finding out about the artist priest and his love for all things to do with the sea.

EARLY DAYS

Born in Southsea and from a naval family, Peter Anson (1889–1975) took a keen interest in ships and seafaring from an early age. Initially, he sketched from photographs, but at the age of 9, during a family holiday at Robin Hood's Bay, he began drawing the 'Fifies' and Zulu Drifters beloved by his mother, a Scots-born watercolourist. Peter attributed his status as a 'Domiciled Scotsman' to her strong maternal influence. She died when he was barely 14 and from this point on, his naval officer father began to have more input into his upbringing.

On one memorable occasion, Peter found himself, age 15, alongside his dad on board the Royal Navy cruiser HMS *Argyll* – sister ship to the ill-fated *Hampshire*, which went down off Orkney in 1916 with Lord Kitchener on board. This was Peter's first experience at sea in a warship and he records that he did not enjoy 'the terrific noise of guns firing' during a naval exercise in the North Sea. Despite this, he was by now smitten with seafaring and regarded himself as a hardened sailor following the experience.

Private tutoring followed and in his late teens Peter enrolled at the Architectural Association School in London's Westminster. Even here, however, he found he couldn't resist drawing maritime subjects. He soon obtained a sketching permit, which allowed him to wander at will, sketchbook in hand, around London Docks. Wapping, Blackwall and the Isle of Dogs became favourite haunts and the Thames river traffic became his subject.

BENEDICTINE MONASTIC LIFE

By 1906, Peter was in touch with the Anglican Benedictine community on Caldey Island, near Tenby, and despite family pressure to follow an architectural career, found himself drawn to the monastic life. In 1910, he tested his vocation as a monk. Following an initial two weeks on Caldey Island, he decided, at age 20, to join the community. Many years later, he wrote: 'I might be giving up the world, but this would not involve abandoning the sea…I don't think that I could have faced the latter sacrifice! It would have been too much to ask!'

For the next decade, Caldey Island became his home. Six miles in circumference and less than a mile long, the island had been home to monks from early Celtic times. In 1906, it was purchased by a Yorkshire-based community of Anglican Benedictines. It is a place of jagged coastal rocks, Atlantic storms and red sandstone cliffs, and it was here that Peter became firm friends with Aelred Carlyle, his monastic superior, who helped him realise the Apostolate of the Sea – a mission to attend to the moral and spiritual needs of those who go to sea in ships.

An article on the subject penned by Peter appeared in *The Catholic Universe* and soon letters began to arrive from all parts of the world endorsing his view that the spiritual welfare of seafarers in general went largely uncared for. One correspondent commented that 'the mercantile marine have no chaplains and the priests in seaport towns are too overburdened with work already to give ships much individual attention'. The *Catholic Times* soon took up the issue and in 1920 the Vatican newspaper *Osservatore Romano* published a condensed Italian translation of Peter's article. Peter had by then moved on to fresh projects.

In what he later realised was an attempt to escape from monastic life and return to the maritime world, he gained permission from the Abbot of Caldey to make a survey tour of the seaports of the UK. He made many sea journeys during this period and travelled from Shetland to the Isles of Scilly. He sailed in dirty colliers and smoke-stained steam trawlers, and at one point spent so long in an Italian cargo vessel that he almost forgot how to speak English.

Peter Anson. (Courtesy Andrew Paterson Scottish Highlander Photo Archive)

In Buckie, he found a fleet of more than 100 brightly painted steam drifters and wondered why no artist had ever painted the confused mass of funnels, rigging and masts. In Aberdeen, he observed 'big dirty, untidy vessels which were a stark contrast to the tidy vessels of the Moray Firth'. Everywhere he travelled he met clergy who he observed had largely given up on ministering to seafarers, whose spiritual needs were then left largely neglected.

The question of what could be done for Catholic seafarers had been the catalyst for the setting up of the Apostleship of the Sea; however, when Peter moved to Portsoy, then to Macduff in 1936, it was soon apparent that the crews of the local herring drifters were made up of men from various persuasions.

'Macduff 1958' by Peter Anson (Courtesy Moray Museums Service)

Methodists, Baptists, Episcopalians and Presbyterians, Brethren, Salvation Army and Catholics were all happy to discuss with him the state of the tide alongside debating the finer points of infant baptism, or the mysticism surrounding the crucifixion.

The painting and the sketching carried on throughout this period, as it did throughout his long life. The Apostleship of the Sea had become an international affair, with annual congresses attracting delegates from up to fourteen countries. By 1936, however, Peter had withdrawn from the official life of the organisation. Indeed, he took great pleasure in the fact that on the occasion of the Congress's meeting to honour his colleague, Arthur Gannon's, seventeen years of devoted work with the award of the pro Pontifice et Ecclesia, he was pointedly busy making a drawing of a Dutch motor cruiser in Banff Harbour, while chatting amiably with its crew.

Peter had, in fact, resigned his position as the Apostleship's organising secretary in 1924, due to health concerns and the feeling that he had visualised the society much as he would visualise a drawing or a piece of writing. Once the piece was completed, he simply wanted to get on with the next project.

A CARAVAN PILGRIMAGE

Many sea journeys followed. Brittany, Vancouver, and a much-needed pilgrimage to Assisi were just some. In 1938 he published *The Caravan Pilgrimage*, an account of his year-long 'Pilgrim Artist' journey by horse-drawn caravan, from Datchet, by the Thames, around Scotland's north-east coastline and back.

For many years, Peter had been contributing a weekly series of drawings to *The Catholic Universe* featuring Catholic churches around Britain. The work involved

'The Horses in Tandem', sketch by Peter Anson (Courtesy Moray Museums Service)

constant travelling by train; he hated road travel, which he found exhausting. One day, he simply decided to divest himself of his copies of both Bradshaw and the ABC Railway Guide and purchased a horse-drawn caravan. Since he knew nothing about horses, his next move was to advertise for a travelling companion who did. From almost 200 applications he chose Anthony Rowe, a young Yorkshireman, who with a lifetime's experience among horses was a qualified farrier. Along with two horses, Jack and Bill, they set off on the year-long journey around Britain, sketching churches and meeting folk along the way. Around sixty of Anson's illustrations of the pilgrimage appear in the book of the tour, including sketches of St Peter's in Buckie, St Mary's in Portsoy and St Thomas's in Keith. Along the way, Jack and Bill enjoyed the privilege of overnight grazing in the grounds of Huntly Castle and Buckie FC's football park, among many other unusual locations.

LIFE AT MACDUFF'S HARBOUR HEAD

In 1936, Peter moved back to Aberdeenshire. He had been living in Norfolk for a while but became weary of what he described as 'the Church of England in its most traditional and un-exciting manifestations'. He had accumulated an intimate knowledge of Scottish seaports, having previously visited most of the forty or so parishes, including in Orkney and Shetland, which then made up the Catholic diocese of Aberdeen, and he knew many of the fifty or so secular priests who served up what he termed 'an undemonstrative type of Catholicism'. The Aberdeenshire and Moray coastline became his home for the next two decades.

Ecclesiastical affairs drifted into the background, as the local fishing communities became his focus and his life. The likes of writers Neil and Daisy Gunn, Compton

Mackenzie and Eric Linklater became firm friends. Indeed, both Neil and Sir Compton were to contribute forewords to his books. Sir Compton had reviewed Peter's writing for the *Daily Mail*, commenting that, 'Mr Anson's books are prized possessions on my bookshelves.' It has been suggested that Neil's *The Silver Darlings* would not have reached publication if Peter had not encouraged the man to publish and be damned. Peter wrote: 'In Scotland … so far as I could discover, I was the only Papist earning a living by literary and artistic work in the vast diocese of Aberdeen.'

Soon after moving into Macduff's Harbour Head, the local parish priest designated Peter's tiny cottage an Apostleship of the Sea 'Service Centre'. As a consequence, a constant stream of mariners of all faiths and nationalities found their way to his door. Alongside the seafarers, there were other visitors in the form of local engineers, farm workers and shop assistants. In wartime, service folk on leave from the armed forces of both the UK and Allied forces frequented his open house. He had begun the Apostleship many years before with the vision of creating a worldwide organisation. At Harbour Head, Peter soon adopted the view that perhaps men, rather than administrative machinery were required; apostles were more needed than an Apostolate.

During this period, he wrote and sketched at a furious pace. He had spent six months in an earth-floored fisherman's cottage in Portsoy, prior to moving to Harbour Head, during which time he completed an academic study titled *The Catholic Church in Modern Scotland*. During his years in Macduff, his writing included classics such as *A Roving Recluse*, *Life on Low Shore*, and the classic *British Sea Fishermen*.

At the behest of the then 'Scottish Nationalist Party', and with a foreword by Neil Gunn, he penned a vitriolic political pamphlet, 'The Sea Fisheries of Scotland – are they Doomed?' which examined in some detail the causes of the decline in the fortunes of the inshore fishing industry in the 1930s.

Books as diverse in nature as *How to Draw Ships* and the 1956 *Official Guide to Banff* followed and are part of his legacy alongside possibly his final scholarly work, *Building Up the Waste Places*, in which he explores the life and work of Aelred Carlyle and Fr Hopkins, each of whom played key roles in the restoration of Benedictine monastic life in the post-Reformation Church.

A founder member of the Royal Society of Marine Artists, Anson published more than forty books and contributed to many more. His artistic output numbers thousands of drawings and watercolours, and many of his books are prolifically illustrated with north-east harbour scenes and pier head paintings.

In 1958, Peter left Macduff and moved to a cottage near Ramsgate Abbey. A further brief stay in Portsoy followed in 1960, and in 1961 he moved to Montrose. He was made a Knight of the Order of St Gregory by Pope Paul VI in 1966, in recognition of his scholarly work, and in 1967 he became the very first curator of the Scottish Fisheries Museum at Anstruther.

His later years were spent back at Caldey Island and finally at Sancta Maria Abbey in East Lothian. He died in St Raphael's Hospital, Edinburgh, in July 1975, and is buried in the private cemetery at Nunraw Abbey.

Aspects of Peter Anson's life remain unclear and some of his personal diaries and correspondence are unavailable to historians until 2040. However, Moray Council Museum Service hold a substantial collection of his work, some of which is on public display at the Falconer Museum in Forres. The Museum Service also holds an archive of his letters and diaries, plus his personal library. Buckie Fishing Heritage Centre and Buckie Library also hold a collection of Peter Anson paintings.

The memorial to Peter Anson in Macduff (© Duncan Harley)

Courtesy of Aberdeenshire writer and historian Stanley Bruce, Macduff sports a sculpture in memory of Peter – but perhaps the most fitting tribute to his life are in the words of an anonymous Buckie fisherman, quoted on the flyleaf of the 1930 edition of Anson's bestselling classic, *Fishing Boats and Fisher Folk on the East Coast of Scotland*:

> Peter's the maist winnerfu' mannie ah ever met, well kent in scores o' ports, a man wi' the sea in's bleed, a skeely drawer o' boats an' haibers an' fisher fowk, a vreeter o' buiks, a capital sailor, an' a chiel ... He's a byordinar mannie.

9

TWO WORLD WARS

Many Scottish First World War memorials are located in town centres, some are on roadsides and a good number, such as that in Oldmeldrum, sit within local churchyards amongst the graves of those lucky enough to have avoided the mud, the blood and the squalor of the European battlefields.

Sited on the summit of Black Hill, the war memorial at Stonehaven overlooks the harbour and can be seen from most parts of the seaside town. Built some years after the end of the First World War the structure, at first glance, resembles a ruined classical temple. Roofless and bounded by rough-hewn sandstone boulders, the Doric columned memorial was designed by local architect John Ellis (1874–1929) and is themed to reflect on the 'ruined lives of those it commemorates'. Unveiled in mid-1923, it was one of the very last war memorials erected in the Mearns and is built on an exposed hilltop site donated by Lady Cowdray – a benevolent local landowner.

Initially the interior was inscribed with the names of the 162 local men who never returned from the First World War – more names were added after the Second World War – and some 4,100 lead-cast letters were commissioned to record the names of the fallen. Alongside recording the names of the dead sons of Stonehaven, the inscriptions around the interior of the monument graphically recall the battles in which they took part. Gallipoli, Jutland, Mons, Marne, Somme, Vimy, Ypres and Zeebrugge appear alongside a poignant but perhaps slightly patronising inscription that reads: 'One by one, death challenged them. They smiled in his grim visage and refused to be dismayed.'

Of course, every community in Scotland was touched by the 'war to end all wars' and as the academic debate continues as to precisely how many Scots died during the course of the conflict, students at Inverurie Academy decided in 2017 to focus on just one man: past student William Reid. As part of an ongoing heritage project titled Hard Vrocht Grun, a Doric phrase translating as 'hard-fought ground', the student team, guided by teacher Jacqui Campbell, discovered that William had been born in nearby Market Place, just yards from the Inverurie War Memorial in the town's Market Square, which today includes his name amongst the roll of the dead. A former Inverurie Academy student,

Stonehaven War Memorial (© Duncan Harley)

William had joined the Gordon Highlanders, a local regiment, in 1914. Rising through the ranks to become a second lieutenant, he died of wounds aged 25 in 1917. Neatly linking the toll that the conflict inflicted both on the battlefield and also within the rural communities who were left to suffer the loss, the Academy team's research culminated in the presentation of a shadow puppet play illustrating the social and economic issues created by the conflict, plus the penning of a Doric ballad dedicated to William.

THE BALLAD OF WILLIAM JOHN REID

In the toun o' Inverurie
Tailor, John, wed Helen 'o
Sealed their weddin' wi' a kiss
And very soon a bairnie'o
William John they ca'ad their bairnie
Born in eighteen ninety-two
Growin' up in Market Place
Aye plenty things for him to do

Colin Coombes – he had the shoppie
Selled his sweeties by the bag
But the time was passin' surely
School was beckonin our lad
Cookin, housework – for the lassies
Joiner work was for the lads
Corridors – baith wide and open
The rector's belt if ye were bad
Our Billy was a 'lad 'o pairts'
A student o' the Arts became
But clouds o' war were gaitherin' o'er him
The 'Gordons' ca'ad him fae his hame
Aff he went tae France and Flanders
Served his country – did richt weel
Made lieutenant – earned some medals
Led his men o'er battle fields
While in France – the battle raging
At Cambrai, wi' tanks and fire
Billy – brave, beyond imagines
Led attack and men inspired
Though hopes were high – a broken bridge
Stopped progress o'er the main canal
And Haig's commands – so ill thocht oot
Meant thoosands there were doomed to fall
Cambrai's mud and open country
Was to lead to his despair
Billy's actions – halted sudden
Almost dead – left lyin' there
They nursed as weel's they could, poor Billy
But in nineteen seventeen
In hospital, in France – our hero
Fae wounds sustained – his life was daen'
And now his memory is recorded
Jist yards from where our lad wis born
His name, inscribed on stane memorial
Where every year we meet to mourn'.

Inverurie War Memorial Gardens (© Duncan Harley)

CONSCIENTIOUS OBJECTORS

There were, of course, many folk up and down the land who objected to serving in the 1914–18 war. Some protesters were ardent socialists who, adhering to the principle that the working classes of the world should unite instead of setting out to kill each other, refused point-blank to fight. And, of course, members of some religious groups were firmly against any taking of human life. Other objectors simply thought that the new war was a capitalist enterprise engineered for the sole purpose of enriching the industrial barons who, having made a fortune from previous wars, were now greedy for further profit on the backs of the 'capitalist dominated masses'. Demonstrations were held around the country, including at London's Trafalgar Square. But in the big scheme of things war fever, backed by Acts of Parliament, meant that those who refused to fight due to conscientious objections were liable to be rounded up and imprisoned for the duration.

By the second year of the war the flow of patriotic volunteers had been reduced to a trickle, possibly due to the realisation that the European adventure generally risked a sentence of death. However, the advent of conscription meant that the right not to serve no longer existed. A Military Service Act was passed by Parliament in early 1916 and although moral objectors were in theory excused from military service, in practice appeals against conscription were held before an often-unforgiving local military tribunal. As a result, some 16,000 men between the ages of 18 and 41 who were unwilling to kill for king and country were sent to work camps to carry out so-called 'work of national importance'. Such duties included the quarrying of slate at Ballachulish, farm labouring in the Buchan fields, and the breaking of stones in a dank quarry on the outskirts of Aberdeen.

Nowadays a long-stay car park catering for holidaymakers and off-shore workers heading abroad via Aberdeen Airport, the Dyce Conscientious Objectors Work Camp opened in late 1916. Initially, it housed some 200 so-called 'Conchies' who were tasked with breaking rocks for roadbuilding. Labelled as moral degenerates by the *Aberdeen Journal*, the camp population was made up of objectors drawn from all walks of life including academics, tradesmen and shopworkers whose only crime was to have refused to don military uniform and stick a bayonet into the 'hated Hun'.

Conditions in the camp were basic. Most inmates were unused to hard labour and lived in leaky ex-Boer War bell tents on-site. Proper sanitation was largely lacking. When it rained, the quarry sides ran with water, which streamed through the campsite. When Walter Roberts, a committed Christian from Stockport, died of pneumonia just five days after admission, the press – who had previously vilified the prisoners as unpatriotic cowards, 'Dyce Humbugs' and degenerates – suddenly took up their case. After some well-placed national publicity by the Peace Pledge Union, a Home Office committee headed by soon-to-be Labour PM Ramsay MacDonald visited the camp. As a result, and following a heated debate at Westminster, the Dyce facility was closed down, ostensibly on cost grounds, and the inmates transferred to prisons across the UK to serve out the remainder of their sentences.

They had spent just a few months as forced labourers at Dyce but, in the true tradition of oppressed people all around the globe, the inmates had managed to set up and publish a camp newspaper – the *Granite Echo*. In the very first edition dated October 1916 an inmate by the name of T.H. Ellison penned a leading article that included the immortal lines:

> Bonny Scotland! And as usual the windows of heaven are open. It appears as though the so called just and merciful God of the civilised nations of Europe – who I think must be taking a day off – is preparing once more to flood the earth, so disgusted is he with the madness of the human race.

BIGGLES FLIES NORTH

A young aviator from Inverurie was killed in combat over Arnaville on 30 August 1918 aged just 21. A lieutenant in 55 Squadron of the Royal Air Force, he lies buried in a small village churchyard near where he fell to earth. An online tribute records that:

> 'Thomas Laing from Inverurie, Aberdeenshire, joined the Royal Flying Corps as a bomber pilot. In April 1918 he went to train at the Royal Air Force (RAF) station in Narborough, Leicestershire, where he learnt how to fly his two-seat biplane day bomber. He wrote to his parents every 4 to 5 days, describing the thrill of flying at high altitudes and finally qualifying as a pilot. On 14 August 1918 Laing went on his first flight behind enemy lines, bombing ground targets in Germany. 16 days later he was shot down and killed.

After his death, Laing's mother received a letter from his girlfriend. It ends: 'I keep on remembering little things he said and did. I just loved everything about him.' Along with the official notification, his mother was to receive his flying goggles, identity bracelet and service medals, along with an official RAF photograph as a memento of her dead son.

Biggles author, Captain W.E. Johns, would have been familiar with such tragedy. Having survived First World War combat with the Royal Flying Corps and spent time as a prisoner of war after being shot down during a bombing raid over Mannheim, Captain Johns was quick to take up the offer of a fishing holiday in the north-east. London, in 1944, was under enemy attack. The Luftwaffe bombers had given way to the unmanned flying bombs, which struck daily terror into the populace. And, commenting that, 'Enemy action has at last forced me to leave my home', the author gladly travelled north to confront the salmon of the River Spey and the River Dee.

Alongside the fishing, the captain penned some dozen or so of his hundred *Biggles* books while staying in the area and he may well have set his tale of kidnap, intrigue and adventure, *Biggles and the Poor Rich Boy*, in a local landscape of which he would have been very familiar. Of course, the southern approach up through The Lecht straddles the modern-day electoral boundaries of Aberdeenshire. Queen Victoria simply hated the area, describing it in her diary as 'the most tumble-down, poor looking place I ever saw', and the nearby upland village of Tomintoul was soundly dismissed in the *Old Statistical Account of Scotland* as being a place where 'All of them sell whisky and all of them drink it'.

Getting to and from Tomintoul is fairly straightforward nowadays, although in the depths of winter and with the snow-gates from Deeside poised to close, it may be quite a different story. From Deeside the A939 snakes its way northwards via the post-Culloden, redcoat stronghold at

Corgarff, before heading up past the Ski Centre. Travellers arriving from the Grantown-on-Spey side have perhaps an easier time of it and their final approach is marked by the Fodderletter Lums. These freestanding roadside stone chimneys closely resemble the gable ends of old cottages; however, the structures were actually built by early road-builders who would place portable shelters around the warm chimney stacks before settling in for the night.

Alongside the *Biggles* connection, the area around The Lecht claims a strong connection to Percy Toplis – better known perhaps as the Monocled Mutineer.

THE ENGLISH DILLINGER

The fictional manhunt described in *Biggles and the Poor Rich Boy* mirrors a very real manhunt that took place in 1920. It was mid-May and Percy Toplis, an out-of-work ex-soldier, arrived in Tomintoul. The villagers and The Lecht Estate workers took pity on him and found him work in the deer forest at Inchrory. Unknown to them, Toplis, a consummate rogue and serial confidence trickster, was a high-profile fugitive on the run following the black-market inspired murder of a taxi driver in far-off Thruxton.

Toplis was a military misfit and something of a loose cannon. He had enrolled in the Medical Corps during the First World War, serving in Gallipoli, Egypt and India. A deserter, he had apparently re-joined the army under an assumed name and is credited with playing a leading part in a six-day long mutiny at an army training camp at Etaples. In 1978, his life story was celebrated in a book published by William Allison and John Fairley that exposed a cover-up in which official military records appeared to deny that any such mutiny had ever taken place.

Following the fatal shooting in Thruxton, Toplis headed north and took up residence in an isolated cottage on the

Lecht, where he began, without permission, to burn the floorboards and tear down a neighbouring farmer's sheep pens for firewood.

This was too much for the farmer and, on 1 June 1920, he enlisted the help of the keeper of the cottage, a Mr McKenzie, and the local bobby. At around 11 p.m., all three men set off to confront Toplis, who was by this time tucked up in front of the open fire. Events soon spiralled out of control. The intention of the policeman had been simply to issue a stern warning, but when challenged, Toplis lured the three unsuspecting men into a narrow corridor at the back of the isolated cottage before pulling out his First World War service revolver and firing point-blank into the huddled group. Both the policeman and the farmer were badly injured, but, by some miracle, McKenzie was unhurt.

Following the shooting, Toplis made off by bicycle to Aberdeen, where he is said to have boarded a south-bound train.

Toplis Cottage (© Duncan Harley)

A CLOSE SHAVE AT ALFORD

Percy Toplis was eventually cornered near Penrith and shot dead following a running fight with armed police. He was just 23 years old when he died.

In 1986, and under the title *The Monocled Mutineer*, the BBC aired a four-part adaptation of the Toplis story, penned by playwright Alan Bleasdale and starring Paul McGann, of *Withnail and I* fame, as Percy. Criticised at the time as being 'riddled with error', the TV dramatisation of the murderer's story not only glorified the so-called English Dillinger, but also failed to use the actual location in which the Lecht shootings took place; instead substituting an ornate, red-roofed cottage of uncertain – and certainly un-Scottish – origin. The genuine location, locally known as Toplis Cottage, lies hidden in full view of passing traffic on the A939, not far from the Lecht Ski Centre. That is, of course, if you know where to look.

A further strange but probably quite accurate account of the monocled mutineer's connection with Aberdeenshire appears in an article published in *Leopard Magazine* some years ago and penned by local author Alastair Stupart. Seemingly prior to his sojourn on the Lecht, Toplis resided for a short while at number 15 Holburn Street in Aberdeen city centre. Shortly before her death, Alistair's aunt, Margaret Mitchel recounted meeting Toplis at the lodging house. The fugitive had rented a room at the back of the Holburn Street property for just a few days and he most probably had his service revolver handy – just in case of awkward callers.

Margaret had mentioned the meeting with Toplis to a good many acquaintances over the years but, until the screening of Bleasdale's take on the story on the BBC in the autumn of 1986, few took much notice of her recollections. Alistair writes that she had paid a call to her aunt Lizzie McDermott, the proprietor of the lodging house. Expecting to be met by her aunt, Margaret was surprised to be met at the door by smart-looking gentleman who promised to tell Mrs McDermott that she had called by. Alistair writes that 'at this time Margaret was a student' – just 20 years of age, and some three years younger than the Holburn Street lodger. Seemingly Toplis 'on leaving Aberdeen made his way up Donside and stopped at Alford for a shave'. Now there's a part of the story that playwright Bleasdale failed to pick up on.

In a final twist of the Toplis tale, Alistair records that when the doomed and by now penniless fugitive stowed away on the south-bound train at Aberdeen's Joint Station at the start of his final journey south, he was soon discovered hiding behind some fish boxes by the guard. 'The train guard clearly did not recognise the country's number one fugitive,' he writes, 'and not only did he not report Percy but he shared sandwiches with him on the long journey south.'

'Perhaps,' writes Alistair, 'this was the final bit of compassion shown to Toplis' before his 'well documented death at the hands of three well-armed police officers and their vigilante-inspired chief constable's son at Penrith.'

Many decades after these tragic events, Police Scotland presented medals and official commendations to the surviving relatives of the victims of Percy's violent rampage on the Lecht.

THAT HITLER WAR

The hills and glens of Aberdeenshire are littered with the wrecks of aircraft that, mainly in wartime, failed to clear the high peaks. In the introduction to the 1976 edition of *The Book of Bennachie*, the late Lord Aberdeen comments that from the roof of Haddo House, he could view this 'stark, frowning sentinel of the Northern flank of the Grampians'.

> When I was a boy, I was convinced Bennachie was a volcano, and always associated it with Vesuvius, which I had read about in my children's encyclopaedia. In later days, when frozen on the plains of Northern France or frizzled in the sands of Egypt, the sound of the piper playing my company march – The Back o' Bennachie – induced the most appalling nostalgia and desire to be back at home again and puff up the Mither Tap. To hell with your Alps, Rockies and Himalaya. Bennachie – the centre stone of the County of Aberdeen is the hill for me.

However, the Bennachie hill range and low-flying aeroplanes do not make for a good mix.

On the very first day of that second war to end all wars an RAF aeroplane crashed into the hill, killing both crew members outright. The Commonwealth Grave cemeteries of the county are filled with the remains of lost servicemen. Many of the lairs contain airmen killed in training accidents over the north-east. One graveyard even contains the remains of a Lumber-Jill killed accidentally during tree-felling operations during 1943. There are, of course, also a good few German graves. Old Dyce Kirkyard holds the remains of two Luftwaffe aircrews who lie buried alongside comrades near the back wall of the Commonwealth Graves section.

A good few myths have been handed down through the generations regarding the impact of the Second World War on the county of Aberdeenshire. One hoary old tale suggests that places such as Inverurie were at the forefront of enemy action during the air-war of 1940–42 but this was not the case. The town was never subjected to enemy action, although the railway repair works must have been a tempting target for the enemy. The Garioch town was garrisoned and became home to both German and Italian POWs, however. And there are a couple of instances where Allied aircraft made emergency landings in the vicinity. In 1943 and in thick fog, an RAF Westland Lysander crash-landed on the land nowadays occupied by Gordon House.

A year or so later a Halifax bomber made an emergency landing at the Kintore dispersal airfield. Suffering from engine failure, the aeroplane was quickly surrounded by local troops while repairs were made. The repaired aircraft took off some eight days later but not before an armoured car charged with guarding it overturned and burned out on a sharp bend at Thainstone, killing all three occupants.

Another oft-repeated wartime tale records that the prisoner of war camp over at Monymusk was populated by Polish prisoners. Nothing could be further from the truth. The camp at Monymusk certainly held Italians, then Germans and perhaps even a few Ukrainian prisoners who had fought on the wrong side, but, in truth, the Poles were our nation's allies. After Poland was overrun in 1940, Poles flocked to the UK to continue the fight against the German occupation from fortress Britain.

Be that as it may, the Monymusk 'Deer Park' prisoner of war camp at one time featured a chapel rivalling the Italian Chapel up at Orkney. The prison chapel at Monymusk survived well into the twentieth century, when it was bulldozed to make way for a housing estate, leaving Aberdeenshire much the poorer. Little or nothing survives above ground to record its existence, although a single black and white photograph of the chapel interior is held within the archives of Monymusk Estate.

AIR RAIDS AND INVENTIVE BULLET HOLES

The suggestion that German bullet holes litter walls of houses on Inverurie's Westfield Drive is, at best, inventive. There are indeed indentations in granite walls of the *circa* 1939 council-built houses all around the Garioch town. George Square and West High Street bear suspicious marks easily mistaken for war damage. But these are most likely tool marks left by the craftsmen who carved out the blocks in the granite workings over at the quarries of Kemnay and Tillyfourie. Aberdeen City, Maud and indeed Peterhead do, however, bear witness to the effects of the Nazi onslaught and tombstones in places such as the Trinity Cemetery in the Granite City still show the effects of blast damage from the Luftwaffe bombing campaign. Although the Garioch town of Inverurie was never bombed, many, now elderly, survivors of those stressful days vividly recall being shepherded by sometimes panicked primary school teachers towards the local bomb shelters when the air-raid siren sounded. That siren now lies neglected and unloved within the clocktower of the Inverurie Town Hall. Abandoned following the cessation of the Cold War of the late twentieth century, the rusting artefact will no doubt end up in the hands of the scrap merchants in a repeat of the fate suffered by 'Julian the Tank', a First World War MK4 tank that sat menacingly atop the Broad Hill at Aberdeen's Beach Boulevard before being recycled as scrap in 1941.

In reality coastal towns such as Fraserburgh and Peterhead bore the brunt of enemy air action. Raiders from occupied Norway could make landfall over the Buchan ports, drop their bombs and make off over the North Sea well before fighters from airfields at Banff and Dyce were able to intercept them. The fishing port of Peterhead suffered at least twenty-eight air raids during the Second World War, with nearby Fraserburgh not far behind with perhaps twenty-six Luftwaffe raids.

Retired railway engineer Joe Strachan recalls being in Peterhead visiting his auntie in 1940. 'I must have been around eight or nine at the time. My aunt and my cousin panicked and I can vividly recall them jumping up and down on the double bed. How that was going to protect them against German bombs, I have no idea. They would have been better off hiding under the bed!' Joe also recalls an attack on a convoy just off Peterhead. 'It was dark and all I could see was what looked like a firework display far offshore but obviously someone was taking a pasting.' On another occasion he returned to his home in Keith with a suitcase filled with tins of sardines which had washed ashore on Peterhead beach following the sinking of a cargo ship. 'A friend found a gun on the beach about the time that the ships were bombed. It was a revolver as I recall. How that thing ended up on the shore is anybody's guess.'

Aberdeen also took a battering, with the press archives of the day recording the carnage in true *Boy's Own* rhetoric such as 'bullets rattling on rooftops like a shower of hail' and the like. More worryingly, modern day Google Map overlays based on the Civil Defence bombing records suggest that unexploded bombs may still lie buried around the harbour area and elsewhere across the city.

AIR ACCIDENTS

Fatal aircraft crashes, often due to accidents in training, were fairly common in wartime and places such as Ballater, Aboyne and Logie Coldstone bear witness to the carnage. In October 1943, for example, a Bristol Blenheim of 526 Squadron based at Inverness crashed on high ground at Morven. Both aircrew were killed in that incident. The pilot, a Welshman, was recorded as Flight Sergeant Douglas Evans and his wireless operator/air gunner was named as Flight Sergeant Charles Baden from Derby.

Another crash, this time of a Wellington bomber on a training mission out of Lossiemouth, occurred in 1942 high up in the hills behind Braemar. A gamekeeper out checking the deer herd at Glen Cluny eventually spotted the tail of the downed aeroplane sticking out of deep snow and alerted the local policeman. The eight aircrew had lain undiscovered for weeks and consisted mainly of New

Zealand, Australian and American servicemen in training. Eventually, some forty-five years after the tragedy, one of the plane's Rolls-Royce Pegasus engines was brought down from the hill and mounted on a granite plinth alongside the Braemar War Memorial as a tribute to the lost aircrew.

The cemeteries around the north-east bear witness to the huge number of aircrew lost in accidents. Estimates vary wildly, but the figure for the whole of Scotland is likely to exceed 8,000 over the course of the Second World War. In addition, some 200 Luftwaffe aircraft crashed over Scotland during the same war. Even after the war's end, RAF crews continued to die. Bad weather, poor judgement and a lack of experience often played a part, alongside, in some cases at least, unforgiving aircraft such as the early versions of the Gloster Meteor.

The 3,430ft-high Carn an t-Sagairt Mòr, 6 miles south-east of Braemar, Aberdeenshire, was the site of an RAF English Electric Canberra aircraft lost in November 1956. Substantial parts of the airframe, including at least one wing and one engine, still remain on the mountain. A report of the time records that:

> The aircraft was seen to climb away for its return to Upwood. At about 19:30 hours (approximately) witnesses from near Braemar heard a jet aircraft pass at an unusually low altitude for that area. One witness saw what must have been the tail navigation light, and the outline of the aircraft as it passed flying south, with the engines sounding normal and on a straight course. A few minutes later the witness saw a flash as it struck the hills.

Both crewmembers were lost.

In more recent times an 81-year-old pilot had a lucky escape when the light aircraft he was flying crashed into a fence at an aerodrome near the village of Insch. The pilot had been flying solo out of Inverness and despite 740 hours flying experience lost control while landing. An aircraft accident report concluded that 'he had lowered full flap earlier than usual and had allowed the speed to decay during the left turn leading to the stall and wing drop'. In this case the pilot survived, although the aircraft, a Druine D62A Condor, was badly damaged in the incident. Ironically, the aircraft had been attempting to land at the airstrips aptly named Runway 13.

The Bennachie hill range was the 1939 location of what were certainly the very first air fatalities involving RAF personnel during the opening hours of the Second World War. The hill has seen two twentieth-century air crashes, the most recent in 1952, when an RAF Gloster Meteor jet fighter on a training flight from RAF Leuchars crashed during a snowstorm into Oxen Craig on 12 February that year. The pilot, Yorkshireman Brian Lightfoot, died instantly on impact and wreckage was scattered over a wide area. One of the aircraft's cannon was retrieved by souvenir hunters and was for a time stashed in a barn over at Oyne before being rediscovered in the 1980s.

The RAF's fleet of Gloster Meteors had what can only be described as a horrendous safety record and records indicate that there were 436 fatal accidents between 1944 and 1986. Some 890 of these aeroplanes were lost during that period over the entire UK, including one piloted by the son of the headmaster of Oyne Primary School. Local writer James Mackay records in a 2012 article in *Leopard Magazine* that 'In the early 1950s fifty Meteor pilots died when their planes dived inexplicably into the ground' and that in 1952 'a Meteor was written off every two days on average and a Meteor pilot was killed every four days'.

The lesser known 1939 air crash on the hill came to prominence in September 2012 when a commemorative cairn was unveiled near the peak of Oxen Craig to commemorate the Meteor pilot along with the crew of an RAF Westland Wallace biplane that had crashed on nearby Bruntwood Tap on 3 September 1939. Around eighty people attended the ceremony, including relatives from both Yorkshire and Canada. As local Air Cadets formed an honour guard, an RAF padre led the service of remembrance and the relatives were guided to the respective crash sites to pay their respects.

The Westland Wallace biplane was equipped to operate as an air-target tug and had been on its way from the Air Observers School at RAF Wigton to an airfield in Easter Ross. On the Dyce to Easter Ross leg of the flight the pilot misjudged his height and, in thick mist, had failed to clear the peak. Both crew, air-gunner Alexander Stewart from Paisley and Canadian pilot Ellard Cummings, were found by the search parties still strapped into the cockpit, leading to speculation that Pilot Officer (PO) Cummings had stalled the plane in the midst of an effort to pull up at the very last moment. The tail-plane was broken off, indicating that the rear of the aeroplane had probably struck the ground first. Both fliers were thought to have died instantly, probably from broken necks, and debris from the crash is still visible on the hillside.

Commemorative plaque, Bruntwood Tap (© Duncan Harley)

In the 1960s walkers on the lower portion of the hill often passed by the rusting nine-cylinder engine from the Wallace wreck, which had been rolled down the slopes of the hill by souvenir hunters. When a local firm of timber contractors removed it to their premises over at Tillyfourie, intending to sell it for scrap, the RAF got involved and repossessed the artefact with the intention of restoring it for display at the RAF Museum at Cosford.

The Wallace aircrew were, of course, taken off the hill for burial. The Canadian pilot, PO Cummings, is buried in the Grove Cemetery in Aberdeen and gunner Alexander Stewart was interred at the Hawkhead Cemetery in his native Paisley.

A 'Find-a-Grave' record relating to PO Cummings reads:

> Ellard was one of the first casualties of WWII, having been killed on the day Great Britain declared war on Germany. He was a Canadian national serving with British forces, namely the Royal Air Force in which he held the rank of Pilot Officer (Pilot) Service No: 40803. He was 23 and the son of James Victor and Edith Fanny Ellard Cummings of Ottawa, Ontario, Canada. Westland Wallace K6028 of 1 AOS, on a ferry flight to 9 AOS flew into hills in bad visibility at Bennachie, near Aberdeen two members of the crew being killed.

James Mackay records in his *Leopard* article that Alexander's father visited the crash site quite soon after the tragic event. He is said to have removed a small section of the aircraft's wooden propeller, intending to carve two scale models of the Westland Wallace airplane in memory of the airmen who are to this day officially recorded as being the very first UK military casualties of the Second World War.

CAPTAIN LIGHTFOOT'S CANNON

In a strange postscript, a letter outlining the fate of Pilot Officer Lightfoot's 20mm aircraft cannon came to light in

May 2017. Apparently a young lad by the name of Hugh Kindness had come across the Meteor wreckage during the school holidays in Easter 1952, just months after the tragedy. Along with some schoolfriends, he had explored the crash site high up on Oxen Craig. 'We wondered,' he recalled, 'if there would be anything to see at the site and so, with Geordie Ross from Hatton, we set out to explore.'

There was little difficulty in finding the place, which at the time was marked by burnt hillside and a wide scatter of debris.

> It looked as if the Air Force had retrieved anything of value, removing engine parts and cutting up larger pieces which were abandoned. We eventually came across a heavy metal tube in the scrub a wee bit away from the site, which seemed to be a cannon. It was pretty heavy and we thought it must be worth a bob or two as scrap. After a considerable debate as to how the three of us, two 14yr olds and an 11, one at 5'6 and two at 5', were to manoeuvre the 6' cannon across the top to the Craigshannoch path down Bennachie. We never seemed to have quite the right heights in the correct place with the rugged terrain and occasionally Gordon got a free swing but we managed it without injury despite dropping it a few times. Why did we do it? It was a bit of a challenge on a lovely spring day but I can't say we were not disappointed to be told that our massive trophy had no scrap value. We often went back to the site in the next few years to watch nature reclaim its own and reflect on the young pilot who almost made it over the top of the mountain.

Jackie Cumberbirch, the Chief Baillie of Bennachie, recalls that, 'The above story was sent to us by Tom and Kit Pawson on May 8th, 2017. Hugh Kindness, one of the boys who retrieved the cannon along with his brother Gordon, is now a retired doctor in Australia. Gordon sadly died in 2006 and is buried in Oyne Kirkyard.'

Tom had bought a farmhouse over at Hillburn near Oyne from Hugh and Gordon's parents in 1975. In 1985, while en route from Hong Kong to New Zealand, he met up with Gordon, who then worked for the Hong Kong and Shanghai Bank. 'When Gordon asked what we thought of the cannon,' he recalled, 'we had no idea of the story or the fact that the cannon was hidden in our stables. On our return, Tom removed a heap of wood from a corner and there was the cannon in pristine condition.'

The aircraft's Hispano 20mm air-cannon sat on display for many years within the Bailies Room at the Bennachie Centre on the slopes of the hill and was later transferred to the Garioch Heritage Museum in Inverurie, in memory of the young RAF pilot who died having missed overflying the 1,732ft high peak at Oxen Craig by a mere 50ft or so.

Although many Meteor aircraft survive in museums, aircraft collections and on static display in public spaces, only perhaps five nowadays remain airworthy worldwide.

HITLER'S HEADMASTER

Freedom of speech is, of course, a very fragile thing. Often hard won, it can be taken away at the stroke of a pen, as an Aberdeenshire headteacher found to his cost in 1940.

Timing is everything. If George Hendry, the local primary school headmaster at Oyne, had just kept his mouth shut for a few more months then in all probability nothing much would have happened to him. He would probably have been dismissed as a crank, at worst, or perhaps even as a well-meaning intellectual. As it was, he became an early victim of the paranoia that gripped the north-east during the early months of the Phoney War.

Various Emergency Powers (Defence) Acts came into force in the early part of the Second World War. Some, such as Defence Regulation 18B, provided a framework for internment of enemy aliens while others, including the Emergency Powers (Defence) Act 1939, gave the state wide-ranging powers to prosecute the war using what nowadays appear to be draconian means. Most aspects of life in the UK came under firm state control, including the 'apprehension, trial and punishment of persons offending against the Regulations'. In short, anyone suspected of acting against the national interest in any manner whatsoever would likely suffer the indignity of a pre-dawn knock at the door.

The village of Oyne was quite distant from the foreign battlefields. It had narrowly escaped being bombed by a German Zeppelin in a previous conflict but in the big scheme of things Oyne was certainly not a front-line target. Nor was it a hotbed of pro-Nazi sympathy. This was 1940, however, and a paranoid nation was smarting from the military defeat in France. The very real threat of invasion loomed and an unforgiving aerial bombing campaign had begun. Towns across the north-east of Scotland had been attacked and coastal shipping had already been sunk by German planes off both Stonehaven and Peterhead. The newspapers were filled with often inflammatory reports of arrests and convictions for the offence of 'Careless Talk'. A meter reader from Oxford was detained after alleging, 'we should be just as well under the Nazis as we are now!' And in Dorset, a policeman was jailed for expressing similar sentiments. In Peterhead a local plumber was fined £5 for the new offence of 'careless talk on the phone'.

Headteachers appear to have been at particular risk of prosecution. Overheard warning pupils that following imminent invasion they would have to resort to eating cats and dogs, a Lanarkshire headmaster found himself before a Hamilton magistrate and at Oyne, local primary school headmaster George Hendry received the dreaded knock on the door on the afternoon of 24 June. The unwelcome visitor was Detective Inspector McHardy of Aberdeen City Police and, after suitable interrogation, Mr Hendry was arrested on matters relating to the Defence Regulations. Lurid headlines followed and public interest in the case was aroused.

EXPRESS

OYNE SCHOO
NOT PROVEN

VERDICT GREETED WITH APPLAUSE

A VERDICT of not proven was given by Sheriff at Aberdeen Sheriff Court to-day on under the Defence Regulations headmaster of Oyne S

Careless Talk 'Phone

Alleged He Said That Ribbentrop Would Be King

Sentenced for Defeatist Talk

Jail For "Chatterbug" Special Constable

Initially there was just the one charge. This related to statements allegedly made in the Union Street grocer shop of Andrew Collie & Co. Witnesses alleged that Mr Hendry expressed the view that Neville Chamberlain had sold the country down the river and should now be placed up against a wall and shot. The King, he had said, was heading off to Canada, leaving the country 'Holding the baby' and Hitler seemingly had more than sufficient torpedo boats to sink the entire British Navy.

Following his arrest and interrogation, Mr Hendry was released on bail of £60. On Monday, 15 July the curious folk of Aberdeenshire queued outside Aberdeen Sheriff Court hoping to witness first-hand what promised to be a very juicy trial. Mr Hendry by now faced four charges – the police had indeed been busy. Alongside the alleged remarks about the King and Hitler's naval prowess, there were allegations of him spreading alarm by remarking on Britain's complete unpreparedness for war. One prosecution witness even termed Mr Hendry a 'fifth columnist' and said that she had ordered him out of her shop, but under cross-examination admitted she had in fact been joking and considered him simply a leg-puller. Another witness told the court she had discussed the war with him on several occasions and that despite their obvious differences in opinion, there was no bad blood whatsoever between them.

Finally, the case against the Oyne headmaster boiled down to one very simple issue – the spreading of defeatist talk in public. In a fine piece of courtroom theatre, Mr Blades for the defence lured the manager of Collie's grocer shop into admitting that the case would never even have been brought had he himself not spread gossip about Mr Hendry's statements to a crowd, which included a policeman, at the public bar of the Royal Athenaeum. The public benches in the courtroom erupted with laughter and the normally punitive Sheriff Dallas indicated that he had heard quite enough. A judicial verdict of Not Proven on all four charges was greeted with loud applause from the crowded courtroom.

George Hendry, a graduate of the University of Aberdeen, became headmaster at Oyne in 1927, having previously taught in Forres. After the trial he returned to his teaching post until his retiral due to ill health in 1963. He died in 1966 aged just 63. In truth, the 1940 trial probably blighted his career. In 1952, just a few years after the courtroom drama, his life was further blighted when a well-loved son died whilst piloting an RAF Meteor jet over the Solway Firth.

DIGGING FOR VICTORY

The notion of growing a few brassicas or indeed some legumes for the kitchen table remains popular throughout the north-east and to make things easier for the kitchen-gardener, Aberdeenshire gardening guru Jim McColl once advocated the keeping of Tamworth piglets as a weed control agent on the vegetable patch. At best guess,

however, after turning over the ground, the cute swine would likely end their days turning over on a spit. The likes of Lawrence D. Hills' classic guide *Grow Your Own Fruit and Vegetables* and the late John Seymour's *The Concise Guide to Self-Sufficiency* had their own take on how to dig for victory, both in wartime and in times of peace. Hill famously concentrated in his writings on the tried and tested four-year rotation of legumes, brassicas, potatoes and root crops; and, apart from recommending that those pesky garden moles are best dealt with by pumping exhaust gas from the garden rotavator into the burrows, he mercifully steered clear of sudden death on the allotment. Seymour, on the other hand, would have agreed with Jim McColl. When he was not busy hoeing his onions or treating the neighbours to a jug of rhubarb wine in the garden shed, he advocated rearing a pig or two for the freezer. Of course, at some points in our history, the home-cultivation of food for the table became something of a necessity.

A COUNCIL PLOT

Wartime rationing and food shortages during both world wars led to a government-sponsored national campaign to Dig for Victory and before very long councils throughout Aberdeenshire and far beyond were encouraging residents to boost national food production by growing their own supplies of vegetables. In more recent years, land reform campaigners claim that many people are looking to reconnect with the fundamental process of growing food for the table.

In an age when there is a disconnect between supermarket shelves and the origin of food items, it is perhaps comforting to realise that there are still some 300,000 allotments in the UK as a whole, with perhaps 10,000 of those being in Scotland. Many remain to this day under council stewardship. In 2017, for example, Aberdeen City Council could boast around 492 council-owned allotment plots located at twenty-one sites across the city.

In Aberdeenshire the figures were much different. While the Scottish Allotments and Garden Society (SAGS) listed a total of eleven active allotment sites in the Aberdeenshire Council area, Aberdeenshire Council listed just five council-managed allotment sites with a combined total of thirty-three plots for the entire county. Indeed, figures for local authority run plots published by SAGS in 2010 suggest that while Aberdeen City Council provided one plot per 493 of the population, Aberdeenshire offered just one plot per 6,827 of the shire population. The SAG's study identified an additional Scotland-wide forty-eight independent sites such Baird Park in Stonehaven where allotment associations rent land directly from landowners, but the report concluded that around 69 per cent of recorded sites were effectively still in local authority stewardship.

Historically, in Scotland, there is a distinction between an allotment garden and an allotment. Confusingly, an allotment garden is defined in the various Allotments (Scotland)

Acts of 1890, 1922 and 1950, as a plot of 'not more than 40 square poles', or about 1,000 square metres. An allotment, however, measured perhaps 4,000 square metres, or 160 square poles, and, alongside the growing of food crops, allotment plots could be used to keep livestock. The legislation was, until quite recently, as clear as mud.

Demand for allotments is strongly linked to periods of food shortage, recession and social change. Following cessation of hostilities in 1919, for example, the Land Settlement (Facilities) Act Scotland encouraged local authorities to provide smallholdings and allotments to jobless returning war veterans who might, if left to starve, pose a direct threat to a government fearful of a Bolshevik-style revolution.

In 1940, food shortages due to the German U-boat blockade led directly to the Dig for Victory campaign. In wartime Aberdeenshire, the national campaign for self-sufficiency led to an offer of rent-free council plots on which patriotic townsfolk could grow their own.

THE FAMOUS DIGGERS OF GEORGE SQUARE

Wartime rationing led to a dramatic increase in demand for agricultural land throughout the county. Marginal land, parkland and golf courses, including the old course at Turriff, were sacrificed to the plough and fallow land was brought into use. Oddly, in October 1941, Inverurie Golf Club actually petitioned the council, requesting that the course be put under cultivation in return for a nominal rent; not out of patriotic duty perhaps, but because membership had declined due to wartime conditions, leaving the club unable to finance ground maintenance. Inverurie's Lands and Parks Committee was the wartime body tasked with inspiring the townsfolk to grow their own and, with Ministry of Agriculture backing via the Dig for Victory campaign, councillors appealed to the public to take up an initial offer of rent-free plots.

Demand proved strong and by March 1940 all thirty-four plots at George Square and Allan Place had been let. Soon after, wasteland at Victoria Street was brought into cultivation. A meeting was held at the local Town Hall, during which Bailie Mitchell, convenor of the Lands and Parks Committee, proposed the formation of an Allotment Holders Association. Benefits would, he explained, include discounts on the bulk purchase of seed, fertiliser and implements. An annual fee would be fixed at 13 pence for the rental of plots measuring 50 square yards.

Advice on cultivation was offered and cartons of seeds were sold at 39 old pence per thirteen varieties, with discounts for OAPs and those on low income. By 1941, demand was such that an additional area of 60 acres between the Lochter Burn and the River Ury was incorporated into the scheme. Known locally as the Docken Hole, this unimproved land had lain fallow for some eighty years. Eventually, around 25 per cent of Inverurie householders registered as plot holders and Bailie Mitchell was driven to announce that 'we have some very famous diggers in George Square ... we must go down and see them and give them some encouragement'. In September 1941, a Victory Garden Show was held in the local Drill Hall on Constitution Street, with prizes awarded for best plot holder and best garden plot. Proceeds of £49 were donated to the Red Cross.

A reporter from the *Bon Accord and Northern Pictorial* was in attendance and recorded, in an extensive article headed 'A Sure Sign', that local man Angus Stuart had exhibited a large V-for-Victory-shaped potato. The Prime Minister of the time, the cigar-wielding Winston Churchill, was no doubt impressed.

In a similar vein, following the outbreak of war in 1939, food production rapidly became the focus of various governmental initiatives designed to harvest produce from the wild and rewrite the cookery books of the nation. Rationing of basic foodstuffs, such as meat, butter and sugar, was introduced and wild harvests such as foxglove leaves, nettles and rosehip berries were collected in season by volunteers, including schoolchildren, encouraged by the Department of Health and on an organised and quite massive national scale.

Government departments, such as the Herring Industry Board and the Potato Marketing Board, advised households to cook with locally sourced produce. In a somewhat Orwellian-style pronouncement, the Food Controller for the north-east of Scotland, Mr G. Mitchell, announced that: 'Scotland's traditional fare, such as tatties, porridge and herring can play a significant part in winning the war.'

New and inventive dishes, such as potato carrot pancake and carrot parsnip pudding, were promoted as both foodstuffs and as health tonics for the young. Carrot marmalade recipes including delicacies such as parsnip leaves and chives were published in the local press and eggless oatmeal cookies vied for prominence alongside carrot and oatmeal soup in the parish magazines. Both oatmeal and carrots were, of course, in good supply, whereas eggs and sugar were scarce. The Gordon Ramsays and the Fanny Cradocks of the day would have been appalled.

Many, if not most, Scottish golf courses were ploughed up to provide agricultural land and even coastal courses, unsuitable for the growing of crops, suffered the indignity of having both sheep and cattle let loose to graze the turf that, not long before, had been lovingly tended by the now khaki-clad greenkeepers. Following a record silage yield in a 1940 trial, Aberdeenshire's Ellon Golf Club gave permission to a local farmer to spread manure on the fairways in order to increase the yield for 1941 and over 20 acres of the Aberdeen Hazlehead course also fell to the plough.

Some golf clubs resorted to humour to combat the enemy, such as this extract from the Richmond Golf Club Temporary Rules, 1941: 'Players are asked to collect bomb and shrapnel splinters to save these causing damage to the mowing machines and in competitions during gunfire, or while bombs are falling, players may take shelter without penalty for ceasing play.'

Many clubs, while willing to support the war effort, looked for ways round the issue of the destruction of fairways and greens and quite a few hit on the idea of producing silage for winter livestock feed. The mantra 'long grass on north-east courses will help to win the war' became common currency until the reality of the shortage of tractors and indeed hands on scythes, struck home. The aptly named Ministry of Fuel and Power had, in any case, urged farmers to conserve tractor fuel in order to 'speed up the tanks' that, by this stage in the conflict, were battling it out in the Western Desert somewhat ironically right on top of the, then unknown and untapped, oil reserves that could easily have fed the North African Campaign war machine.

The classic dilemma of a Keynesian economy at war was simplified into a simple Guns or Butter equation and the Churchillian propagandist 'Kitchen Front' was born. The term 'Kitchen Front' was, of course, more applicable to the efforts of those, mainly women, who actually worked in the household kitchens up and down the land. As the UK stay-at-home mothers tried to make some sense of new ingredients such as powdered eggs and corned beef in order to feed their families, a multitude of female agricultural workers slaved backstage to produce the raw materials for the nation's diet. In the big scheme of things, of course, the state had already taken over and in a nod to the warehousing of bully beef during the Aberdeen Typhoid scandal of later years, the state-run warehouses of the 1940s began to swell with the grain and the meat from the prairies of the Americas. The wartime food supply crisis led eventually to some forty-three vast refrigerated meat and fish storage units being built during 1941 alone, plus another forty or so grain stores being completed soon after to feed a population well below post-Brexit twenty-first-century levels. State management of food production and state-run food distribution was central to the war effort just as surely as was the state management and manufacture of munitions, steel helmets and Spitfires.

THE WOMEN'S LAND ARMY

The Women's Land Army (WLA) had been a creation of the Board of Agriculture in the early days of the First World War. Established in 1915 when Britain was short of both agricultural and industrial labour, the Land Army eventually peaked at an estimated quarter of a million female agricultural labourers towards the end of that war. In the Second World War the Land Army was re-established under the command of the Ministry of Agriculture and Fisheries (Minagfish for short) and headed by Lady Denman. As an ex-chairman of the Women's Institute Sub-Committee of the Agricultural Organisation Society and founder of the quaintly named 'Smokes for Wounded Soldiers and Sailors Society', or the SWSSS as it was more commonly known, she had some experience of both agriculture and the essentials required to run a wartime economy.

At the start of the Second World War, Lady Denman – daughter of Weetman Pearson (later Baron Cowdray), the oil magnate and newspaper baron – at first asked for volunteers, but when those were slow in coming forward, the noble lady was advised by the Ministry of Agriculture and Food that conscription would be required in order to fulfil food production quotas. The Ministry of Supply appointed local co-ordinators to take charge of local recruitment and one such official, a Mrs Cook of Ballater, proposed that the daughters of gamekeepers and smallholders would make ideal recruits. In charge of recruitment for the Alford and Deeside areas, Mrs Cook was to be quoted in the local press as advising that 'farmers now realise how well these girls have done in tackling general farm work'. However, she doubted whether the demand for such labour could be met given the often conflicting priorities of the wartime economy. By mid-1944 the Women's Land Army had over 80,000 recruits nationwide, whose ranks had by then been supplemented with Italian and German prisoners of war.

Officially disbanded on 21 October 1949, the WLA remained largely ignored in the history books and in line with the Bevin Boys and the Arctic Convoy seamen the WLA received scant recognition for many decades until NFU former president Jim McLaren, whose mother Katherine had been a land girl in Aberdeenshire, recognised that there was no permanent memorial to the WLA anywhere in the UK. Jim then set up a committee to rectify the situation and within three years over £50,000 was raised.

And so it was that on 9 October 2012 Prince Charles unveiled the Women's Land Army Memorial – designed by Yorkshire artist Peter Naylor – at Clochan with the words: 'It gives me enormous pride to be able to join you on this exposed hilltop to pay a small tribute of my own to all of those remarkable Land Girls who did so much when the country was under threat.'

The Women's Land Army memorial (© Duncan Harley)

NORTH-EAST COASTAL DEFENCES

In the mid-twentieth century, fear of invasion from German-occupied Norway led to the construction of beach defences along the entire east coast of Scotland, and while the cliffs around places such as Stonehaven made seaborne landings unlikely, bays and inlets were seen as vulnerable to enemy assault, often offering an easy exit inland that might be exploited by invading troops. Accordingly, a defensive line running from the mouth of the Cowie Water all the way inland as far as Braemar, was constructed. It was the period of the so-called Phoney War and state-sponsored paranoia headed by a state-controlled press called for extreme defensive measures along the threatened beaches of the north-east.

Barbed wire, minefields and concrete emplacements were hurriedly constructed and beaches all along the Aberdeenshire coastline bear the scars to this day. Alongside the pillboxes and the coastal gun batteries, a series of defence lines was built. Based on First World War principles, it was supposed that coastal invaders, faced with an impenetrable trench-system, could be held or perhaps thrown back into the sea. This outdated military thinking failed to take into account the lessons of the Spanish Civil War and completely misunderstood the post-First World War advances in mechanised warfare. Fortunately, the military planners of the Second World War home front were never challenged by an invading army versed in the theory and practice of Blitzkrieg.

One of the three defensive lines or 'Stop Lines' constructed in the Aberdeen area, the Cowie Defence Line, was by far the most extensive in comparison to the defences along the Rivers Dee and Don. Exploiting the natural features of the landscape, pillboxes and anti-tank blocks were placed at strategic points, such as road and rail bridges, and the riverbanks were cut away in many places to form impassable barriers intended to divert and slow down enemy mechanised troops long enough to allow counter-attacks to be organised. Additionally, an armoured train manned initially by Polish soldiers ran up and down the east coast rail network on a daily basis. Intended as a back-up for the troops on the shores, the train carried both reinforcements and light artillery and the vainglorious hope was that it would provide fire support to the local coastal defenders until relieved by more powerfully armed mechanised ground forces. Never to be used in anger, the Aberdeenshire armoured train was later taken over by a Dad's Army-style Home Guard platoon who continued the patrolling schedule begun by the Poles.

Although much of Stonehaven's Second World War concrete defence work appears to have been incorporated within the town's twenty-first-century flood defences, the area around Urie House retains several classic structures from those troubled times. Identified by military planners as a vulnerable crossing point over the river, the two old bridges on Urie estate were obstructed by anti-tank blocks, with covering fire from a granite-built pillbox. The riverbanks were steepened and a moveable railway block was placed on the Glenury Viaduct. Fortunately, these defences were never tested, although the town did experience the direct effects of twentieth-century warfare on more than one occasion. In January 1940, for example, the cargo ship SS *Gowrie* was bombed and sunk just 4 miles offshore and in the August of that year, in a highly unusual action during which a force of German seaplanes attacked a coastal convoy just south of the town, the SS *Highlander* returned to port in Aberdeen with the burnt-out remains of an enemy bomber on its foredeck. Anti-shipping mines often floated ashore on the east coast and although most were defused and made safe, this was not always the case. Stonehaven's oldest building, the Tolbooth, fell victim to one such device in 1944, when a massive explosion severely damaged its roof. It was not until 1963 that the building was fully restored, prompting a visit by the late Queen Mother to perform an official reopening.

Writer, primary school teacher and local historian Elizabeth Christie penned two books about Stonehaven. In her local history *The Empty Shore*, she records the story of Cowie. 'For most parts,' she writes, 'Cowie Village is an attractive group of houses clustered close by the northern shore of Stonehaven Bay.' Cowie, now a sea-front suburb of Stonehaven, seemingly once boasted a defensive castle built and funded by no less than Scottish king Malcolm Canmore (1058–93), and William the Lion (1165–1214) once gave 'the lands at Cowie' to the 'Red Friars of Aberdeen'.

Coastal defences. (© Duncan Harley)

In Elizabeth Christie's volume *Haven Under the Hill*, she records the later history of the seaside town. Alongside tales of the Barclay family and the southern visitors who came on holiday during the Glasgow Fair, she describes the military matters of the 1880s. Apparently a detachment of Gordon Highlanders arrived in town to complete a route march from Edinburgh. Young men, no doubt inspired by recent victories in the Anglo–Zulu Wars, were treated to a splendid ball at Ury House attended by many distinguished guests. In the evening, she records that 'each guest was rewarded with a tin of tobacco, the lid bearing a picture of Ury House, plus a pipe and a box of matches'. Next day the Gordons set off on their way to Banchory with their heavy luggage being taken on ahead by rail.

The Zulu Wars were to take an awful toll on Aberdeen's Gordon Highlanders, and in years to come the young men of the regiment were to be sacrificed on the poppy-strewn plains of Europe not just the once, but twice more.

Miss Christie, as her pupils referred to her, seldom shared her feelings with her Dunnottar primary class. But her charges still recall her tears each year when, on the anniversary of the death of a brother who perished amongst the dense blue clay of Flanders fields, the entire class would be asked to recite John McCrae's poignant poem 'In Flanders Fields'.

In Flanders fields the poppies blow
Between the crosses, row on row,
That mark our place; and in the sky
The larks, still bravely singing, fly
Scarce heard amid the guns below.

We are the Dead. Short days ago
We lived, felt dawn, saw sunset glow,
Loved and were loved, and now we lie,
In Flanders fields.

Take up our quarrel with the foe:
To you from failing hands we throw
The torch; be yours to hold it high.
If ye break faith with us who die
We shall not sleep, though poppies grow
In Flanders fields.

John McCrae, of course, had experienced the carnage at first hand. A Canadian doctor and artillery commander, he penned the poem in memory of a dead friend – Lieutenant Alexis Helmer, killed on 2 May 1915 in the gun positions near Ypres by counter-battery fire. He made many revisions to the poetic lines and is said to have never been completely satisfied with the verses. Indeed, some reports suggest that he tried to destroy the writing only to have it rescued by a fellow soldier who had experienced the same suffering and loss.

Having almost survived the entirety of the war, Major McCrae died of meningitis in a military hospital in the French seaside resort of Wimereux in January 1918, perhaps unaware that his tribute to that dead comrade had become a propagandist national anthem for the selling of War Bonds.

10

HEALTH MATTERS

Leprosy was until quite recently an incurable, horribly mutilating and extremely contagious disease. According to recent World Health Organisation estimates, around 180,000 people worldwide are currently infected with the disease. Even today, over 200 people are diagnosed with leprosy in the US every year, mostly in California and in Hawaii. There was even a recorded case in Ireland a few decades ago.

Leprosy probably died out in Scotland several hundred years ago, although there are a few sites in Aberdeen associated closely with the disease. The Grampian Fire and Rescue Service headquarters, for example, was constructed on the site of an old leper house just off Kings Crescent. Bede House in Old Aberdeen also has associations with leprosy and may well be situated on the site of a lepers' hospital.

St Fittick's Church on Nigg Kirk Road reputedly features what is commonly held to be a leper's window, although this is now in some dispute since the disease may in fact have died out in the area well before the small opening in the northern wall was actually formed. St Fittick was of either Scottish or Irish descent, according to which account you adhere. He may have been a son of the Dalriadan King Eugene IV and is often said to have been brought up on Iona. Equally, he may have been born into a noble Irish family. What seems certain though is that as a young man he lived in France. Unfortunately, the facts surrounding his provenance are all a bit hazy.

Tradition suggests that he was sent by the Roman Catholic Bishop of the French diocese of Meaux to deliver Christianity to the Picts in the north of Scotland. Along the way, he was reputedly swept overboard from his ship during a storm and washed ashore at Aberdeen's Nigg Bay, where he is said to have refreshed himself from a local spring before founding the church of St Fittick's on the site. Some accounts differ from this story and one even goes so far as to claim that he was actually thrown overboard by the superstitious crew who simply wanted rid of the man and considered him a bad omen. The truth, of course, will never be known.

What is certain is that St Fittick is the patron saint of gardeners, having apparently performed a miracle by single-handedly clearing a large area of forest for cultivation. Mysteriously, he is also the patron saint of Parisian taxi drivers. St Fittick's Day is usually celebrated on 30 August in the UK and is celebrated a day later in Ireland. St Fittick's Church in Nigg is also where William Wallace, or at least the relic of the man that was sent to this corner of Scotland, is said to be buried. A counter-claim suggests that the Wallace relic, if indeed it ever existed, is actually interred within the walls of Aberdeen's St Machar Cathedral.

'PYREXIA OF UNKNOWN ORIGIN'

May 2014 saw the fiftieth anniversary of the terrifying outbreak of typhoid in Aberdeen City. Headlines such as 'Typhoid in Bully Tin' would put many Aberdonians and indeed consumers around the globe off eating corned beef, some even to the present day. The series of events that led to the Aberdeen Typhoid Epidemic was, however, global in nature and involved significant governmental failure.

The outbreak began quietly on 16 May 1964 when two university students were admitted to Aberdeen Royal Infirmary with a diagnosis of 'pyrexia of unknown origin'. They had been fevered for several days and on 20 May bacteriological test results confirmed a diagnosis of typhoid fever, by which time the two unfortunates had been transferred to the City Hospital, which housed the local fever and isolation unit at the time of the outbreak. Further cases quickly emerged and by the end of May there were 238 suspected cases being treated at various hospitals throughout the north-east.

By the end of the epidemic a total of 540 cases had been admitted with suspected typhoid, with 507 being confirmed as having the disease, including eighty-six children under the age of 12. There were three deaths plus an additional eight linked cases treated elsewhere, including one in Canada. Indeed, so-called 'typhoid contact' was a feature of the outbreak and statistics compiled by Dr William Walker indicated that the 507 confirmed cases derived from a mere 309 city households out of a total of around 58,000 households in Aberdeen City.

On 17 June 1964 the epidemic was deemed officially over and although many patients would continue to be treated after this date, the number of fresh hospital admissions had dwindled to single figures, with no new cases being diagnosed after 31 July. There have been several such public health epidemics since 1964, with the 1996 Lanarkshire E.coli 0157 food poisoning outbreak ranked as being amongst the most devastating. A total of twenty-one people died in the Lanarkshire outbreak after eating contaminated meat supplied by a butcher's shop in Wishaw, Lanarkshire. In 1998, Sheriff Principal Graham Cox concluded after a two-month inquiry that the shopkeeper, John Barr, had been ignorant of food hygiene procedures and had also deceived food inspectors. Despite vigorous denials, the William Low supermarket in Aberdeen, which was identified as being the most likely initial source of the 1964 typhoid epidemic, also suffered from poor hygiene procedures resulting in contamination of shopworkers' hands, utensils and surfaces, and leading to contaminated products being sold for consumption by the public.

BULLY BEEF

In this instance it was proven that a 6lb can of Argentinian corned beef had been the source of infection and that not only had the meat been subject to poor hygiene procedures, but it had also been stored in an unrefrigerated shop window in summer heat, leading to a marked increase in the rate of bacterial growth. Although many associate corned beef with corn, it is in fact a salt-cured product treated with corns of salt. Used in many cultures as a means of preserving meat, it has been variously labelled salt beef, bully beef or in India and Bangladesh as hunter beef.

A staple for troops on active service due to its non-perishable nature, it has been produced on an industrial scale for over 200 years. Although consumption decreased markedly in the period after the Second World War, there is still significant global demand for the product, much of which is manufactured in South America. In the early 1960s, the UK imported around 200,000 tons of beef from Argentina annually, amounting to around 14 per cent of the nation's requirements, with a significant proportion being canned corned beef intended both for current consumption and for governmental stockpiling in case of nuclear war.

By 1963 typhoid had all but been eradicated in the UK. Public health education combined with improvements to public utilities such as chlorination of water and treatment of sewage had borne fruit. There had been outbreaks such as that at Croydon in 1937, where, after investigation, it was found that a sewage worker who was a carrier of typhoid had been allowed to work on the water supply during a period when the water purification plant was out of action. The resulting outbreak affected 344 people, of which forty-three died.

Aberdeen was no stranger to the disease either. An outbreak in the city's Woodside district had killed six out of a total of thirty-five cases in 1935, with the source being identified as a local shop selling cooked meats. However, the notion that Argentinian corned beef might be a source of the disease seemed to break new ground. Unless, that is, one takes into account the Harlow typhoid outbreak of June 1963. After extensive testing of public water and sewage supplies proved negative, the source was suspected to be a local butcher's shop selling imported corned beef. However, the government of the day was not keen to publicly blame the Argentinian factories. Notwithstanding, the Ministry of Agriculture and Fisheries and Food (MAFF) began to look at the source of the canned beef and attention soon spotlighted issues to do with the cooling of the cans during manufacture. Seemingly the possibility of the bacteria surviving the high temperatures used during production was almost zero. However, since the Argentine factories concerned with the production of British-imported corned beef routinely used untreated river water in the cooling process, suspicion soon focused on the possibility of contaminated water entering through burst can seams and causing bacterial contamination of the contents.

A LEPER COLONY

Following a further outbreak of typhoid at South Shields in June 1963, Enoch Powell, then Minister of Health, was asked in Parliament, 'How many of the recent outbreaks of typhoid fever had been traced to Argentine corned beef and what steps had been taken to warn the public?'

The Health Minister's reply was simply 'None'. Politics had triumphed and public health had become secondary. The government officials concerned with overseas trade were not keen to blame the Argentinian factories until a diplomatic solution to the issue of untreated river water infected with raw sewage could be found. There was no immediate action apart from a recommendation that a mere two MAFF meat inspectors should visit a total of sixteen meat-producing countries including the Argentine over the following few months. The government were quite clearly not prepared to risk upsetting a trading partner and, worse still, stocks of potentially infected corned beef stored in UK warehouses could continue to be released into the UK food chain despite the possible risk to public health. A further outbreak took place at Bedford in October 1963 but still officials stalled on measures that might have prevented further outbreaks.

The Argentine factory identified as the probable source of the infected cans had agreed to introduce chlorination of cooling water by early January 1963, but MAFF held warehoused stocks of almost 2.5 million cases of the now suspect corned beef dating back as far as 1953. Eventually, much of the suspect stock would be shipped abroad for consumption elsewhere, along with a recommendation that it should be reprocessed. This process of disposal would take several years to complete.

The effects of the political indifference to the spectre of further typhoid outbreaks were to have far-reaching consequences for the city of Aberdeen and indeed the entire north-east of Scotland. Local revue comedy group 'Scotland the What?' parodied the episode in humorous terms: 'I can mind the typhoid epidemic at its worst, we never washed wir hands unless we did the lavvie first.' For many in the north-east, however, it was no joke.

Initially the Scottish press were unaware of the 1964 Aberdeen outbreak but as the numbers of hospital admissions grew it became obvious that an epidemic was in progress. Headlines proclaimed a 'City Under Siege' and the situation was not helped by the proclamation of the then Medical Officer of Health, Dr MacQueen: 'We're not a leper colony! End this hysteria!'

THE HIDE OF A RHINOCEROS

His subsequent advice to both Aberdonians and holidaymakers alike to avoid swimming or paddling in the sea led to a local paper headlining on 'Beach Bombshell' and pretty effectively killed off any short-term prospect of the return of the lucrative 'Glasgow holiday trade' to the beach seafront area.

Described by a colleague as 'a bulldog with the hide of a rhinoceros', Dr MacQueen's strategy of innovative traditionalism has been seen by some as an attempt to protect and extend his department's services. He was judged to have made excessive use of the media and to have turned the outbreak into an event approaching a national crisis. Indeed, the Milne Report into the handling and course of the epidemic commented that 'we consider that the methods used by the Medical Officer of Health' were 'not wholly justified'.

By the end of May 1964, the MOH was advising the national press that Aberdeen was now 'a beleaguered city' and suggesting that Aberdonians should not venture outside the city boundaries. Outsiders should 'stay away', he said. Public baths, youth clubs and sports clubs closed down for the duration and the Aberdeen Police Pipe Band had to cancel an appearance in Renfrew. Even the normally sedate *Sunday Times* newspaper got in on the act with an exclusive, which claimed that the Granite City's image as a clean modern city was erroneous. Aberdeen was in reality a city suffering chronic housing problems and Victorian sanitation. Such histrionic comment only served to deepen the crisis. The news of the epidemic was reported around the globe, with one Spanish periodical reporting that the streets of Aberdeen were littered with rotting corpses waiting to be thrown into the sea.

Although the tourist trade was first to suffer, with hotels being particularly hard hit, there were significant effects felt all over the north-east. Caravan sites and hotels began refusing bookings from Aberdonians, butcher meat and fresh produce firms saw their customers sourcing goods elsewhere rather than risk buying from a city under siege. The Elgin-based wholesale fruit firm Reeve Ltd found it necessary to announce that none of their merchandise was coming from Aberdeen and a grocer in Forres told customers that it had cancelled all supplies from the city and now only sourced from firms in the south of Scotland.

TRAWLER DEFECATION

The local transport firm, Alexander's Bus Company, reported a marked decrease in ticket sales with some services running virtually empty and at one stage a panic ensued when an Aberdeen butcher in Thistle Street was wrongly identified as being the source of the outbreak. Paranoia reached a peak when the catch of an Aberdeen trawler was seized after the skipper became ill with suspected typhoid. The matter was discussed at the daily crisis meeting in the council offices.

After some deliberation, during which a prominent public health scientist pointed out that 'unless the crew are in the habit of defecating in the hold, there is no scientific reason to suppose that the fish pose a health risk,' the catch was duly released for public consumption. For patients and relatives the experience was more serious, however.

Placed in isolation wards and uncertain as to when or even if they would be allowed home, patients had to endure weeks of treatment separated from friends and family. Stories of patients communicating with relatives through locked windows are common and as one Oldmeldrum ex-patient recalls, 'I couldn't understand why my father and mother weren't allowed at my bedside; later when I was allowed up we would talk at the ward window, which was, of course, closed. This went on in my case for about five weeks. Luckily I have not had any long-lasting effects from the illness but it must have been really hard for the younger children.' Many locals have similar stories to tell.

Compared to the human cost of the Lanarkshire E.coli outbreak's twenty-one deaths, Aberdeen's typhoid epidemic's total of three fatalities pales into insignificance; however, the after-effects rumbled on for years. Some businesses never recovered and jobs were lost. In addition, tourism never really returned to previous heights and the local economy faltered until the bonanza that was North Sea oil came to the rescue.

In the wake of the outbreak there were inquiries at both local and national level, the Milne inquiry being perhaps the most influential. In summary, the Milne Report squarely identified the source of the infection as being infected corned beef imported from the Rosario factory in the Argentine and further stated that there was no evidence that the infected meat had come from government stockpiles. The fact that the UK government stockpiles of corned beef at the time contained large quantities of Rosario cans was seemingly not an issue for Milne and his report concluded optimistically that 'where canned meats are produced under satisfactory hygienic conditions – they will be free from any health hazard'.

It took almost ten years for the existing emergency corned beef stocks in UK government-run warehouses to be disposed of. The main method of disposal was the exporting of the suspect food to markets abroad. Not only had the citizens of Aberdeen eaten the evidence from the initial source of the outbreak but over the years subsequent to the Milne committee's deliberation, the unsuspecting citizens of many other countries consumed much of the remaining evidence.

But back to the events of 1964. We frequently hear complaints from restaurateurs and publicans about the strict food hygiene rules and the cost of training staff to adhere to the standards required by environmental health inspectors. It is most unlikely that food inspection or hygiene courses will cause either E.coli or leprosy, but they may prevent us from getting sick.

Had Dr MacQueen been more astute in handling relations with the media back in 1964, then perhaps Aberdeen would now be the tourist destination of choice for the *cognoscenti* of Europe, in addition to being the Oil Capital of Europe.

Compared to the human cost of the Lanarkshire E.coli outbreak, Aberdeen's typhoid epidemic pales into insignificance, except that we still remember it as if it were yesterday. The dubious legacy of Dr MacQueen's 'hide like a Rhinoceros' lives on, more than fifty years later.

11

SHINY WHITE WINDMILLS

Renewables such as wind, solar, hydro-electric and biomass accounted for around 30 per cent of the UK's electricity production in 2017 and wind power, both onshore and offshore, accounted for almost half of the total. But, as always, there are those who dispute the science. One such man, a golf magnate, hotelier and sitting US President, tried and failed to interfere with Scotland's offshore renewables energy policy.

Despite legal challenges by Donald Trump, both the landscape and the waters around the north-east are nowadays populated with wind farms. Forests of shiny white turbines sit spinning on the hillsides along the A96 at the Glens of Foudland and vast fields of offshore turbines feed energy through undersea cables to the National Grid. A recent report on the Vattenfall North Sea offshore wind farm development claimed that one single spin of a turbine blade could produce enough energy to power an average home for a whole day, or alternatively generate sufficient power to drive a golf buggy from Balmedie to John O'Groats. Once completed, Vattenfall is expected to supply enough electricity to power some 80,000 houses. A company spokesman commented that the project boasts some of the most powerful wind turbines in the world and went on to claim that, 'This project is all about transferring Aberdeen from an oil hub to a global energy hub.' Indeed, many coastal settlements in the county are looking to offshore power generation in a bid to obtain clean energy and new hi-tech jobs.

Modern-day Fraserburgh lays claim to being the largest shellfish port in Europe and is also a major white fish port with a busy commercial harbour. Alongside the landings of fish, the town is home to a number of modern fish processing factories and a bustling fish market. However, recent contraction within the fishing industry has led the Harbour Board to seek out new markets. With a population currently hovering around the 12,500 mark, there have been moves to attract companies servicing the new offshore Klondike to the coastal town.

In March 2014, Moray Offshore Renewables Ltd (MORL) gained the consent of the Scottish Government to construct and operate a 1.116MW offshore wind generation farm 13 miles offshore in the outer Moray Firth. To be known as the 'Telford, Stevenson and MacColl Offshore Windfarms', the project's sixty-two giant turbines will require significant onshore facilities to support operation and maintenance for decades to come. With around 330 jobs in prospect, the Harbour Board has recently begun talks with MORL aimed at providing berthing, dry dock and ship lift repair facilities to the project.

With the town's Kinnaird Head holding the record for the highest sea-level windspeed ever recorded on the UK mainland – 142mph on 13 February 1989 – the success of the offshore generating project seems pretty much guaranteed despite US opposition.

OFFSHORE RENEWABLES

Fergus Ewing, then Scottish Energy Minister, on announcing the go-ahead for the Vattenfall scheme told journalists that he was optimistic:

> Offshore renewables represent a huge opportunity for Scotland, an opportunity to build up new industries and to deliver on our ambitious renewable energy and carbon reduction targets. The proposed European offshore wind deployment centre will give the industry the ability to test and demonstrate new technologies in order to accelerate its growth. [It] secures Aberdeen's place as the energy capital of Europe.

In response to the announcement of the go-ahead by the Scottish Government, Donald Trump, head of Trump International Golf Club Scotland Ltd, said, 'We will spend whatever monies are necessary to see to it that these huge and unsightly industrial wind turbines are never constructed.' The rhetoric seemed familiar. Prior to his appearance in front of the Scottish Government Economy Energy and Tourism Committee in 2012 he was quoted as saying that there was not a shred of evidence that turbines benefit the environment.

During a press conference following this hearing he told journalists that, 'If Alex Salmond was smart, he would stop right now because what he's doing to Scotland is terrible. This is the same thing as al-Megrahi when they let him out of prison because he would die in two weeks. And guess what, he was running around the park last week.' Scottish Green MSP Patrick Harvie was quick to label Trump's comments as sick, saying, 'Trump has sunk to a new low', and went on to claim that, 'Trump's organisation has already trashed a unique environment on the coast of Aberdeenshire and trampled on the rights of local people'.

In reference to al-Megrahi, Dr Jim Swire, whose daughter Flora died in the 1988 Lockerbie bombing, said the Lockerbie murders had 'no place in a confrontation between an entrepreneur who is interested in making money in Scotland and the government'.

This was not the first time the Trump organisation had attracted criticism. Complaints about a press advert had been upheld by the Advertising Standards Authority (ASA) with the organisation being warned 'not to exaggerate the number of turbines likely to be installed or the possible consequences of the Scottish Government's plans to use wind turbines'. This followed a regional press advert dated 19 September 2012 for an organisation titled 'Communities Against Turbines Scotland' and was headed 'Welcome to Scotland!' above a photograph of broken and rusty wind turbines with text stating, 'Alex Salmond wants to build 8,750 of these monstrosities – just think about it! Join us in Edinburgh for a march and a rally.'

Inevitably, the ASA was again deluged with complaints about the new advertisement. In conclusion, the ASA stated that: 'The ad must not appear again in its current form. We told Trump International Golf Club Scotland Ltd not to make claims unless they could be substantiated with robust evidence and not to use misleading imagery.'

Interestingly, Mr Trump claims Scottish ancestry. He has been quoted as saying that he is half Scottish: 'My mother, Mary MacLeod, is from Stornoway on the Isle of Lewis. She grew up in a simple croft until she landed in Manhattan at the age of 20 and her first language was Gaelic. When I saw this piece of land I was overwhelmed by the imposing dunes and rugged Aberdeenshire coastline.' Be that as it may, the white shiny windmills are here to stay whether the incumbent US President likes it or not.

In a further new initiative, Aberdeen has been chosen as one of five sites in Scotland to trial an energy capture system based on giant kites, each the size of a Wimbledon tennis court. The system, backed by a study carried out by London's South Bank University, involves tethering two huge kites to a ground-based winch which in turn drives a generator. The technology is reckoned to have the potential to significantly undercut the costs of other renewables and is backed by Scottish Enterprise and Royal Dutch Shell to the tune of around £7m. Now imagine, if you will, one of these giant kites hovering just above the 13th hole at the

Trump International Golf Links over at Balmedie. At best guess the embattled presidential golf course owner might be seen to be a wee bit under par.

Mind you, the late Doric poet Bob Smith had a take on both Trump and turbines. Over the years, Bob penned around 200 poems in the Doric tongue and not a few of them included a pre-Presidential Donald within the subject matter.

One such poem, first published in the *Aberdeen Voice*, includes the immortal lines:

The Donald's bocht a golf resort
Doon on the Ayrshire coast
A'll get ti host The Open
Wull noo be his prood boast
Thirty Five million he did spen
He got Turnberry fer a snip
Es o coorse micht mean
Interest in Menie taks a dip
Jist cast yer myn back
Fin winfairms he did detest
The mannie made a vow
In Scotland he'd nae mair invest
Fit ti mak o ess U-turn
As he cums crawlin back
Bein economical wi the truth
The chiel still his the knack
Hud on a wee meenitie tho'
It micht nae be plain sailin
The spectre o affshore winfairms
Cwid yet hae Trumpie wailin
Marine Scotland it his reported
Aboot a site jist oot at sea
Far ye cwid plunk win turbines
They'd be richt in Donald's ee
Fergus Ewing says ess plans
Fer noo are aff the radar

Yet fair refused ti rule oot
Returnin ti them later
If a winfairm cam ti pass
Wid The Donald then renege?
Or wid he maybe in a rage
Blaw up yon Ailsa Craig
At Doonbeg he'd ti stop some wark
Did he nae hae richt permission?
He can tho' noo gyaang ahead
Maybe efter a new submission?
Micht Donald hae fresh concerns
A snail in Ireland is protectit
Bi speecial environmental laws
An ess canna be correctit
Trump says he's gyaan ti wark
Wi environmentalists an sic fowk
If he'd deen aat ower in Menie
He micht nae bin classed a gowk
Noo ere's nae doot the mannie
Oot the news he winna bide
Wull we next aa be hearin
The bugger's bocht the River Clyde ...

Bob, or Smithie as he was known to his colleagues, had a habit of getting right to the heart of the matter.

MY LADY OF THE WILDERNESS

Of course, it's not just billionaires who loath the white shiny windmills. Aberdeenshire's Clashindarroch Forest is home to both turbines and wildcats. When Swedish energy giant Vattenfall announced plans to expand the existing Clashindarroch wind farm near Huntly, campaign group Wildcat Haven raised objections. Citing statistics suggesting that the forest was home to around thirteen of the estimated thirty-five remaining endangered Scottish wildcats left in the wild, they raised concerns that the species would be driven even nearer to extinction if the clear-fell required to build the new wind farm was given the go-ahead. With headlines screaming 'Wildcats at risk of being wiped out by windfarm', a petition launched by the campaign group quickly gathered over 200,000 signatures.

In a bid to conserve one of the last habitats of the threatened mammal, the environmental activist group is offering plots of Clashindarroch forest land for sale. Seemingly, for a mere £30 per square foot, purchasers can not only protect the endangered moggies but can style themselves Lord or indeed Lady of the Wilderness and, in doing so, can establish a safe haven for a species teetering on the very brink of extinction.

Both Vattenfall and Forest Enterprise Scotland, however, disagreed with the protest groups' environmental stance, citing a track record of sensitive and sustainable species management. Vattenfall project manager Alison Daugherty went on record to say that 'the wildcat population in Clashindarroch Forest is unaffected by our four-year-old operational windfarm', while a spokesperson from Forest Enterprise pointed to their important role in carrying out actions that 'conserve wildcats and other important species'.

The thirteen resident wildcats of Clashindarroch have yet to make their views public and many supporters doubt that the threatened mammals can afford the £30 fee required to secure ownership of their forest haven.

Of course, the big challenge for renewable energy is storage. It's all very well generating a few trillion megawatts of power in a high wind over the North Sea but, unless you are prepared to stay up all night washing clothes and watching daytime TV, then all is to little avail. While the likes of Tesla claim to have found an automotive solution, the problem of storing this rich fruit of the wind is still just a smidgeon out of reach. But if Project Batwind is to be taken even remotely seriously, then the storage issue needs some urgent attention.

Fifteen miles off Peterhead, Equinor and Masdar Electricity have pioneered a ground-breaking system involving five wind turbines, which generate some 30 megawatts of electricity, connected to an onshore battery system estimated to have the ability to store sufficient electricity to power some 128,000 smartphones. Considering that charging an iPhone costs slightly less than £5 per year, cynics are of the opinion that the Batwind company's claims are way off the mark. Despite this, the new storage system is being pioneered along the Aberdeenshire coastline, with Peterhead chosen as an experimental landfall.

12

BLACK GOLD

In his book *Oil Strike North Sea*, Aberdeenshire geologist and oil industry insider Mike Shepherd looked critically at the boom and bust cycle of North Sea hydrocarbon exploration. As global oil prices remained volatile and the UK government recorded its first loss in forty years from North Sea oil and gas production, Mike examined in some detail the huge discoveries on the Forties Field in 1970, the share price crash of Black Monday 1987, and the human cost of North Sea exploitation in terms of accidents including, of course, the Piper Alpha disaster.

While on a geological field trip to Skye during 1978, Mike had witnessed first-hand the construction of the Ninian Central platform. Fabricated in Loch Kishorn and weighing in at an impressive 601,000 tons, the concrete and steel structure was believed at the time to be the largest man-made structure ever to be moved across the surface of the earth. 'The North Sea proved to be a new frontier for the oil companies ... they had been offshore before ... but never in waters quite so stormy or so deep,' he writes.

The first oil was pumped ashore in 1975 from the Argyll oil field. Both the city of Aberdeen, often referred to as the Oil Capital of Europe, and the surrounding towns and settlements in the shire have subsequently benefited greatly from several decades of oil and gas prosperity following the initial discovery of commercially viable reserves some nine years earlier. However, volatile twenty-first-century oil prices and consequent job losses have impacted the local economy in recent years. Indeed, newspaper articles claiming that 'Another 5,500 people working in the North Sea oil and gas industry in Aberdeen are set to lose their jobs within the next decade, according to Scotland's national skills agency' have become common currency.

North Sea oil platform (© Margaret MacLean)

However, the casual visitor to the region could be forgiven for assuming that the area is still in the boom stage of oil exploration rather than in what is undoubtably an unremarkable slump phase. Supply vessels still clog the harbour while dozens more can be seen queuing offshore awaiting their turn to onload a new cargo. Indeed, now that Google Street View includes a virtual reality tour of the Cygnus platform – the single largest offshore gas production facility in the North Sea and some 93 miles from the nearest highway – it seems to many that the jobs and the offshore lifestyle are here to stay.

Almost every town in the shire can boast at least a few oil-related businesses supplying technical expertise and components to the offshore industry. On the face of it, the local economy appears to be thriving. New-build housing developments dot the countryside, while on the outskirts of Aberdeen state-of-the-art oil-related office blocks spring up at a reassuring rate. New infrastructure such as the £995m Aberdeen bypass and a new £300m conference centre suggest a booming local economy and local authority projects such as the refurbishment of the Aberdeen Art Gallery and Music Hall, at a combined cost of some £40m, suggest at least a degree of civic prosperity. But behind the scenes all is not well, as a plethora of business failures graphically illustrate. Despite a splendid effort on the part of the city fathers, pound shops and bookmakers nowadays haunt the high streets of the Granite City. Pub failures and restaurant closures abound and at the time of writing both the shire and the city are plainly on the back foot, at least for a wee while. With an estimated twenty billion barrels of oil still remaining to be extracted off Britain's shores, industry leaders are warning that unless 'some serious exploration is done, we are looking at extracting just 50 per cent of the remaining reserves'.

It is estimated that income from North Sea oil and gas accounted for around 10 per cent of UK Treasury revenue during the latter part of the twentieth century, and local billionaire and oil doyen Sir Ian Wood might just agree. He recently expressed his regret that Aberdeen didn't benefit more from the North Sea oil boom. Aberdeen-born Sir Ian, speaking to the *Sunday Times Scotland*, was quoted as saying that 'Even with a degree of foresight, it's very difficult to handle growth and keep control of a boom economy.' He continued, 'we were all aware that as the oil and gas grew, our traditional industries – fishing, agriculture and tourism – suffered'. The industry that brought prosperity to the north-east is now starting to look at decommissioning as a future revenue source with the offshore assets and subsea structures of the Curlew field high on the list of prospects. Just 130 miles south-east of Aberdeen, Curlew is expected to reach what the industry terms 'its economic limit' sometime in 2019, and plans are well on track to remove the floating platform and its undersea umbilical piece by piece.

OCCIDENTAL'S INFERNO

Oil and gas extraction has always had both a financial and a human cost and the public parks and the cemeteries all around the north-east can testify to this. July 2018 marked the thirtieth anniversary of what became known worldwide as the Piper Alpha Disaster and, at a service held in the Queen Mother Memorial Garden at Aberdeen's Hazlehead Park, a lone piper played a lament, which was followed by a minute's silence. Civic figures including Lord Provost Barney Crocket mixed with oil executives plus friends and family of the 167 oilmen who lost their lives in the world's worst peacetime offshore oil disaster.

The oil business is undoubtably dangerous for those at the cutting edge. The rewards are high but the cost in lives can be prohibitive. For example, a grassy grotto in Johnston Gardens just off Aberdeen's Viewfield Road hosts a memorial to the sixteen men – two pilots and fourteen oil workers – killed in a 2009 North Sea helicopter crash just 11 miles off Peterhead. The chopper apparently suffered catastrophic mechanical failure and plunged 'like a torpedo' into the North Sea, killing all on board. The commemorative memorial is in the form of an obelisk carved from black granite and inscribed with the names of those who died on the Bond-operated flight, which was on its way back to Aberdeen from the Miller oil platform. Eight of the victims hailed from the north-east of Scotland, seven from the remainder of the UK, and one, 39-year-old Mihails Zuravskis, was from Latvia. There have been several more helicopter disasters in the intervening years, each with varying degrees of severity. Piper Alpha was, however, a disaster on a much grander scale.

The Piper Alpha oil platform was by all accounts a truly massive man-made structure. Operated by Occidental Petroleum, it weighed in at some 14,000 tons and was around two and a half times the height of the Statue of Liberty. Producing up to 125,000 barrels per day, it stood on four giant sea-legs each around 90m in length and could accommodate 224 workers. Designed primarily to extract oil, the rig routinely sent gas onshore via an undersea pipeline and burned off any surplus via a giant flare stack. On the fateful day of 4 July 1988, the rig exploded in flames when a pump feeding the burning gas flare began to leak then caught fire. As the platform burned out of control, there was confusion. Firefighting equipment failed, breathing apparatus was not to hand and workers found that lifeboats could not be reached due to the flames. On the seabed, diver Gareth Parry-Davis had been de-gritting part of the undersea structure and suddenly became aware of a bright light from above followed by a series of concussions that reverberated through the water around him. Over the intercom, the diving supervisor instructed Gareth to ditch his tools and make his way back to the diving bell as fast as possible. When the bell was raised, Gareth saw from the expression on his co-workers faces the severity of the situation. Every employee on the platform had a designated lifeboat and the diving team were no exception. However, the lifeboat station allocated to them lay some 40ft above the dive module and the stairway leading skyward was blocked by thick black smoke and flames.

Eventually some nineteen of the diving team, led by dive superintendent Stan MacLeod, escaped by climbing down knotted ropes to sea level where a standby vessel, the fishing boat *Silver Pit*, picked up all but one of them. But higher up on the rig many more men remained trapped within the accommodation module awaiting a rescue that would never come.

The accommodation module stood directly above the main drilling area, the source of the inferno, and the workers inside had been instructed to await rescue by helicopter. They were not to know that the single helipad had been destroyed in the explosions that rocked the burning platform. In fact, the accommodation module was to become a horrific deathtrap for all those seeking sanctuary inside. By 3 a.m. the next morning just forty survivors had been lifted from the sea, some of whom had resorted to jumping 30m or so into the burning North Sea. The accommodation module with the bodies of 122 men inside was recovered from the seabed twelve weeks later. In all 167 men had died that night, including the two crew of the fast rescue boat *Sandhaven*, who were last seen heading off into the inferno to pick up survivors. As is so often the case with disaster at sea, thirty of the dead have no known last resting place.

An inquiry into the disaster, headed by Lord Cullen, concluded that both engineering failings and a lack of basic safety protocol had led directly to the deaths. The Piper Alpha platform was said to be ageing, rusting and unstable and much was made of the claim that safety alarms were routinely ignored. In the light of the Cullen Report findings, Health and Safety law underwent major changes in the UK.

Survival training became mandatory and protective clothing compulsory. On top of that, offshore installations nowadays are required by law to have quick escape routes to lifeboats. Amongst Lord Cullen's remarks was a tribute to the heroism of the diving crew: 'These personnel were efficiently and intelligently led and their orderly evacuation owes a lot to the presence of mind of Mr MacLeod and Mr Barbour, the latter of whom perished when making his escape to sea.' Stan MacLeod was later awarded the Queen's Award for Gallantry for his heroic actions on that harrowing day.

The Piper Alpha Memorial in Aberdeen's Queen Mother Rose Garden within Hazlehead Park was unveiled by Her Majesty the Queen Mother on 6 July 1991 and incorporates an urn containing ashes of victims of the tragedy. Selecting lost heroes for the Unknown Warrior grave at the Whitehall Cenotaph must have been hard indeed, but selecting ashes from amongst the 167 lost North Sea oilmen for interment within the Piper Alpha Memorial must have been even more difficult.

Modelled along the lines of the Commando Memorial at Spean Bridge, artist Sue Jane Taylor initially set about designing a plaster moquette for submission to the city council. Her proposal was accepted. Funding came from many sources and, alongside a good few private donations from survivors' groups, the £100,000 target was eventually reached following a contribution from the Scottish Office of £40,000. The three human sculptures featured on the memorial were made at The Scottish Sculpture Workshop at Lumphanan.

As artist Sue Jane Taylor later recalled:

> The roustabout figure which faces west represents the physical nature of many offshore trades. The survival-suited bronze figure facing east represents youth and eternal movement and the central bronze figure represents maturity. In his left hand he holds a pool of oil. His right-hand points to the ground, indicating the source of crude oil.

Curiously, there are claims that the oil rig's owners, Occidental, declined to contribute to the Hazlehead memorial sculpture and may even, according to some commentators, have gone so far as to discourage other oil exploration companies from picking up the tab on the basis that such a lasting monument would be a constant reminder of the failings of the industry in their duty of care to the workforce. PR objectives had perhaps triumphed over corporate guilt.

One survivor, Bob Ballantyne, famously went so far as to write to the Occidental CEO, Dr Armand Hammer, suggesting that the company might consider donating the scrap value of the burnt-out accommodation module to the memorial fund. Unsurprisingly perhaps, Dr Hammer did not respond.

The Piper Alpha memorial sculpture in Aberdeen's Hazlehead Park (© Duncan Harley)

In a moving rededication ceremony held at Hazlehead in July 2013, oil industry Chaplain Gordon Craig joined with around 800 attendees to commemorate the twenty-fifth anniversary of the awful event. Following a flypast by an RAF Sea King helicopter, politicians, industry representatives, relatives and, of course, those who were there at the time laid wreaths and read out the names of all of the dead. The weather was bright and sunny, just as it had been all those years ago when the roustabouts, the deep-sea divers and that multitude of offshore tradesmen paid the ultimate price of oil.

At the thirtieth anniversary rededication ceremony – led by Revd Gordon Craig, Chaplain to the Oil & Gas Industry – in July 2018, the names of all 167 victims were read out to a crowd of around 1,000. The Lord Provost of Aberdeen, Barney Crockett, said of the event: 'The service was profoundly moving. Everyone in Aberdeen and beyond recognises the incredible sadness of the Piper Alpha tragedy.'

The thirtieth anniversary ceremony was, of course, quite surreal since many of those present intimately knew the men who had died on that calm summer day back in 1998. As the names of the dead were read out, folk broke down in tears. Some were relatives but a dwindling few had actually been witness to the worst accident of its kind in the entire history of offshore oil exploration.

ABOUT THE AUTHOR

DUNCAN HARLEY has written extensively about the history and the mythology of the north-east of Scotland.

Although not born and bred in Aberdeenshire he considers the county his adoptive home. He worked for a time at a well-known street newspaper before turning to freelance writing and blogging. Feature writing now takes up much of his time alongside the penning of both theatrical and literary reviews. Duncan lives in rural Aberdeenshire with his cat Lucy and is surrounded by a huge pile of other people's books. At weekends and holidays, he and partner Janice Rayne like nothing better than to explore the history and the landscape of the north-east of Scotland.

BIBLIOGRAPHY

Aberdeen Voice. *Various editions 2010 onwards* (Community owned digital newspaper – editor Fred Wilkinson)

Aitken, Margaret. *Six Buchan Villages* (Self-published *c.* 1975)

Aitken, Margaret. *Six Buchan Villages* (Scottish Cultural Press 2004)

Anderson, James. *The Black Book of Kincardineshire* (Johnston 1853)

Anson, Peter. *The Caravan Pilgrim* (Cranton 1938)

Bailies of Bennachie. *Bennachie Again* (William Culross & Son 1983)

Balfour, Bernard. *Secrets, Stories, Memories and Stones* (Cranstone 1993)

Barclay, Gordon. *If Hitler Comes* (Padstow 2013)

Braemar Gathering Annual – Various (Dee Publishing)

Burnett, Allan. Duff House at War (Aberdeenshire Council, unknown date)

Chorlton, Martyn. *Scottish Airfields Vol.3* (Countryside 2010)

Christie, Elizabeth. *The Empty Shore* (Bruce 1974)

Christie, Elizabeth. *The Haven under the Hill: The Story of Stonehaven* (Bruce 1977)

Cunningham, Tom. *Your Fathers the Ghosts* (Black & White 2007)

Davidson, John. *Inverurie and the Earldom of the Garioch* (A. Brown & Co. 1878)

Duff, David. *Queen Victoria's Highland Journals* (Lomond Books 1998)

Ferguson, David. *Shipwrecks of North East Scotland* (Aberdeen University Press 1991)

Gordon Forum for the Arts. In Celebration of Inverurie (Culross – unknown date)

Grampian Regional Council. *A Historical Walk Around Peterhead* (School Resources Department 1998)

Hamilton, Sheila. 'What's in a name' (Aberdeen Journals Ltd 1986)
Harley, Duncan. *The A–Z of Curious Aberdeenshire* (The History Press 2017)
HMSO. The Public Enquiry into the Piper Alpha Disaster. (HMSO 1990)
Inverurie Academy. *In Time of War* (Culross Printers, unknown date)
Isherwood and Welsh. *Walking Deeside, Donside and Angus* (Clan Books 2004)
Kilbride-Jones, FE. *An Account of the Excavation of the Stone Circles at Loanhead of Daviot* (HM Office of Works)
Leopard Magazine. Various editions (Aberdeen University/Judy Mackie editor)
Mackie, Alexander. *Aberdeenshire* (Cambridge University Press 1911)
Marren, Peter. *Grampian Battlefields* (Mercat Press 1990)
McConnachie, Alex Inkson. *Donside* (James G. Bisset 1900 edition)
McGinty, Stephen. *Fire in the Night.* (Macmillan 2008)
McKean, Charles. *Banff and Buchan: An Illustrated Architectural Guide* (Mainstream 1990)
Meldrum, Edward. *Aberdeen of Old* (Rainbow 1993)
Morgan, Diane. Various including Footdee (Highland Printers Inverness 1993)
Osborne, Mike. *Defending Britain* (The History Press 2011)
Pittock, Murray. *A New History of Scotland* (Sutton Publishing 2002)
Porter and Williams. *Epidemic Diseases in Aberdeen and the History of the City Hospital* (Polestar 1971)
Robb, William. *Victorian Scenes* (Keith and District Heritage Group *c.* 1980)
Rowe, Anthony. *The Brown Caravan* (Cranton 1935)
Shepherd, Ian. *Exploring Scotland's Heritage* (Her Majesty's Stationery Office 1986)
Shepherd, Mike. *Oil Strike North Sea* (Luath Press 2016)
Shepherd, Mike. *When Brave Men Shudder: The Scottish Origins of Dracula* (Wild Wolf Publishing 2018)
Smith, Robert. *Discovering Aberdeenshire* (John Donald Publishers 1998)
Smith, Robert. *Land of the Lost* (Birlinn 1997)
Smith, Robert. *The Road to Maggieknockater* (Birlinn 2004)

Stewart, Alan. *North East Scotland at War* (Self-published 2018)
Swan, Eddi. *His Majesty's Theatre: One Hundred Years of Glorious Damnation* (Black & White Publishing 2006)
Tacitus. Agricola (Various AD 83)
Taylor, Les. *Luftwaffe over Scotland* (Whittles 2013)
The Bailies of Bennachie. *The Book of Bennachie* (William Culross & Son 1976)
The Buchan Heritage Society. *Heirship '94* (The Buchan Heritage Society 1994)
Thomson, Arthur. *The North-East* (Aberdeen University Press 1930)
Toulmin, David. *Straw into Gold* (Impulse Books Aberdeen 1973)
Toulmin, David. *The Tillycorthie Story* (University of Aberdeen 1986)
Vallance, Hugh. *The Great North of Scotland Railway* (David St John 1991)
Watt, Brian. *Old Stonehaven* (Stanlake Publishing 2000)
Watt, William. *A History of Aberdeen and Banff* (William Blackwood 1900)
Webster, Jack. *Jack Webster's Aberdeen* (Birlinn Books Ltd 2007)
Wood, Sydney. *The Shaping of Aberdeenshire* (SPA Books 1985)
Wyness, Fenton. *Royal Valley* (Reid 1968)

INDEX